Leveson Francis Vernon-Harcourt, Jules Gaudard

Foundations

Leveson Francis Vernon-Harcourt, Jules Gaudard

Foundations

ISBN/EAN: 9783337059293

Printed in Europe, USA, Canada, Australia, Japan

Cover: Foto ©ninafisch / pixelio.de

More available books at **www.hansebooks.com**

FOUNDATIONS.

BY

JULES GAUDARD,

CIVIL ENGINEER.

Translated from the French by

L. F. VERNON HARCOURT, M. A.,
Member of Institution of Civil Engineers.

REPRINTED FROM VAN NOSTRAND'S MAGAZINE.

NEW YORK:
D. VAN NOSTRAND, PUBLISHER,
23 Murray and 27 Warren Street.
1878.

PREFACE.

This essay, from the pen of an eminent continental engineer, was presented, after translation into English, to the Institution of Civil Engineers of Great Britain by L. F. Vernon Harcourt, M.I.C.E.

It was reprinted from the "Proceedings" of the Institution in *Van Nostrand's Magazine*, Vol. XVIII.

The importance of the subject and the eminence of the author justify the belief that, in the compact form of the Science Series, it will be an acceptable addition to engineering literature.

FOUNDATIONS.

The Author proposes to give a description of the principal methods resorted to in making foundations. Although these methods are applicable, in general, to every sort of construction, they possess a special importance in the case of large bridges, on account of the greatness of the load, the instability of the soil, and the amount and flow of water to be contended with. It is not sufficient, moreover, that the bed of the river and the ground upon which the foundations of a pier rest are firm, they must also be secured against scour, as only hard rocks are unaffected by a rapid stream. To ascertain the nature of the soil on which foundations are to be laid borings are generally taken, but they sometimes prove deceptive, owing to their coming on some chance boulders, or upon some adhesive clays which, without being firm, stick to the auger, and twist it, or arrest its progress, and the specimens brought up, being crushed and pressed together, look firmer than they really are. To remedy these defects some engineers have adopted a hollow boring tool, down which water is pumped and reascends, by an annular cavity between the exterior surface of the tool and the soil, with such velocity that not only the detritus scraped off by the auger, but pebbles also, are lifted by it to the surface. This process is rapid, and the specimens, which are obtained without torsion, preserve their natural consistency.

On stiff clay, marl, sand, or gravel, the safe load is generally from 55 to 110 cwt. on the square foot, but a load of 165 to 183 cwt. has been put upon close sand in the foundations of the Gorai bridge, and on gravel in the Loch Ken viaduct and at Bordeaux. In the bridge at Nantes there is a load of 152 cwt. to the square foot on sand, but some settlement has taken place. Under the cylindrical piers of the Szegedin bridge in Hungary, the soil, consisting of clay intermixed with fine sand, bears a load of 133 cwt. to the square foot; but it was deemed expedient to increase its supporting power by driving some piles in the interior of the cylinders, and also to protect the cylinders by sheeting outside. Cylinders, moreover, sunk to a considerable depth in the ground, possess a lateral adherence, as is evident from the weights required for sinking them, which adds greatly to the stability of the foundations. Taking into account this auxiliary support, the loads of 159 and 117 cwt. per square foot, at the bottom of the cylinders of the Charing Cross and Cannon Street bridges respectively, are not excessive. On a rocky ground the Roquefavour aqueduct exerts a pressure of 268 cwt. to the square foot.

Foundations may be classed under two heads:—(1) Ordinary foundations, on land, or protected from any considerable rush of water; (2) Hydraulic foundations, in rivers, or in the sea.

ORDINARY FOUNDATIONS.

When the ground consists of rock, hard marl, stiff clay, or fine sand, the foundations can be laid at once on the natural surface, or with slight excavation, and with horizontal steps where the ground slopes. At the edge of steep descents, with dipping strata, it is necessary to find layers which will not slip, or, if there is such a tendency, to strengthen the layers of rock by a wall, especially when it is liable to undergo decomposition by exposure to the air, or to use iron bolts uniting the layers of rock. On ground having only a superficial hard stratum resting upon a soft subsoil, buildings have sometimes been erected by merely increasing the bearing surface, and lightening the superstructure as much as possible; but generally it is advisable to place the foundations below all the soft soil. On an uneven surface of rock a layer of concrete spread all over affords a level foundation. Sometimes large buildings have been securely built on quicksands, of two great thickness to be excavated, by the aid of excellent hydraulic mortar, and by excavating separately the bed of each bottom stone. Such a building will be stable if its pressure on the foundation is uniform throughout, and if it is placed sufficiently deep to counterbalance the tendency of the sand to flow back into the foundations. Instances of this class of foundations are to be found in sewers built on water-bearing sands, which sometimes give rise to as much difficulty as foundations built in rivers; as for example in the net-work of London sewers, and in the Metropolitan railway. The flowing in of sand with the water in pumping, and consequent undermining of the houses above, was prevented in these cases by constructing brick or iron sumps for the pumps in suitable places, surrounding them by a filtering bed of gravel, and using earthenware collecting pipes, thus localising the disturbance. In the construction of the Paris sewers, where the water-bearing strata could not be excavated on account of the running in of the sand, the upper portion only of the culvert was first constructed (Fig. 1). A little trench was then dug

Fig. 1. Fig. 2.

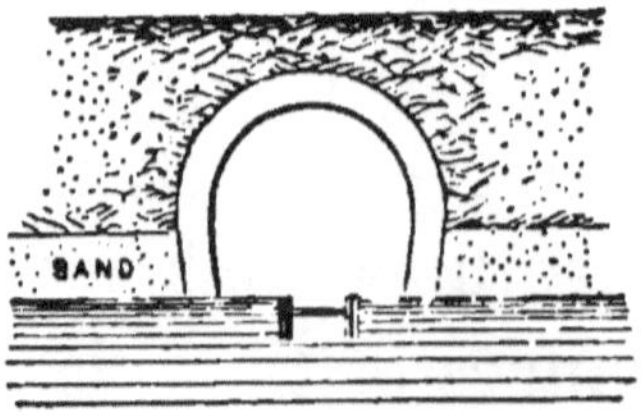

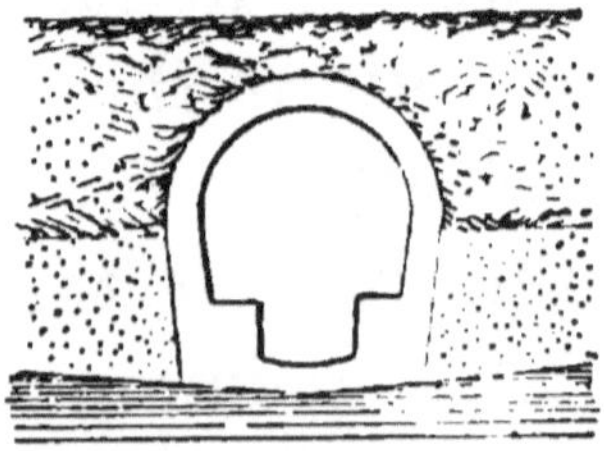

SEWERS IN PARIS

out at the bottom, each side being supported by interlaced boards, and this trench was then pumped dry in lengths of about 110 yards at a time. When one length was dry, a second row of boards was beaten down on the top of the first row, and at last it was possible to excavate the soil in lengths of thirteen feet, carefully shored up, in which the lower portion and the invert could be constructed, completing the section of the culvert (Fig. 2). In this manner a culvert, nine feet ten inches wide, twelve feet six inches high, and 2,050 feet long, was constructed in eighty-five days. The excavations for a sewer at Grenoble were executed from below upwards, in order to insure a continuous flow of the water, and the sides were built as the excavation proceeded, a trench supported by boards conveying the water, and the invert was begun when the piers were finished, commencing at the upper part; semicircular troughs of cement having been placed at the bottom of the excavation to afford continuous drainage, over which a layer of quick-setting concrete was deposited (Figs. 3 and 4).

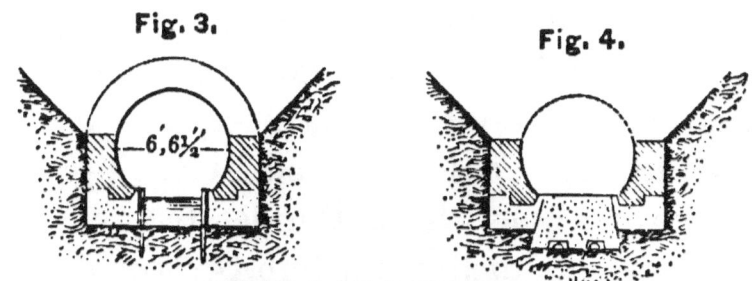

SEWERS AT GRENOBLE

One means of reaching a solid foundation without removing the upper layer of soft soil is by piling, but piles are liable to decay in many soils. In Holland, buildings on piles of larch, alder, and fir have lasted for centuries, whilst in Belgium large buildings have been endangered by the decay of the piles on which they rest. Sometimes columns of masonry support the superstructure, but, being placed farther apart than piles, it is necessary to connect them with arches at the surface for carrying the walls. Piers, however, of viaducts supporting a heavy load must be carried down in one mass to the solid ground, as in the case of the viaduct of Otzaurte, on the Rio Salera in Spain, where it was necessary to get through sixty-five feet of silty clay to lay the foundations of a pier thirty-one feet long by thirteen feet wide. In order to avoid getting out so large an excavation in one piece, a well was dug, four feet wide, and extending across the whole width, thirteen feet, of the piér, so as to divide it into two equal portions (Fig. 5). A chamber, nine feet ten inches high, was then driven at the bottom, like a heading, as far as the limits of one-half of the foundation of the pier, and built up with masonry.

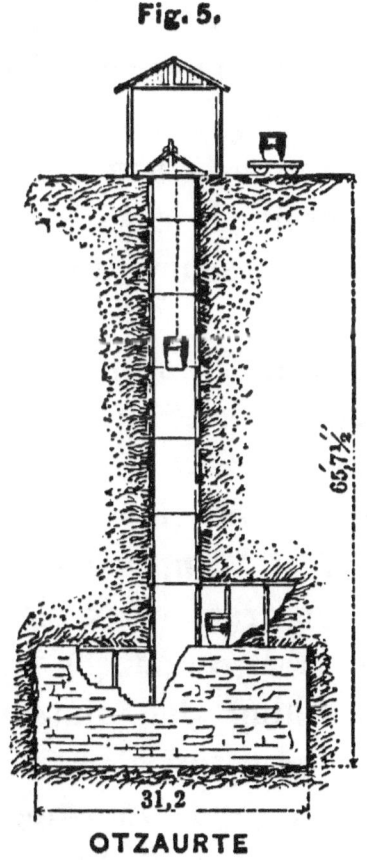

Fig. 5.

OTZAURTE

The other half was similarly dealt with, and the excavation and masonry were carried up in successive lifts of nine feet ten inches. The central well served as a means of access for pumping out the water, for the removal of earthwork, and for the supply of materials.

To avoid the difficulty and expense of timbering deep foundations a lining of masonry is sometimes sunk, by gradually excavating the ground underneath, and weighting the masonry cylinder, which is eventually filled in with rubble stone, concrete, or masonry, and serves as a pier.

In India a similar system has been followed for centuries for sinking wells. The linings are made in radiating courses of bricks or stones; the first length, from five to ten feet high, being put on a circular wooden framework placed on the surface of the ground. Very fine sand is used for filling the joints, except for the two or three top courses, which are laid in mortar, and the whole construction is tightly bound together. It is then gradually sunk by a man inside undermining it, and another length is placed on the top. As these operations are generally conducted in the silty or sandy bed of rivers which become dry in summer, there is no running water to contend with, but water percolates into the excavation, and then the natives use a "jham," by which they remove the earth from under water. Although the external diameter of the wells has been sometimes limited to five feet, the advantage of larger dimensions in securing a vertical descent has been always recognized. At the Western Jumna canal rectangular linings were adopted with advantage. At the Solani aqueduct hollow cubes with sides twenty feet long, and at Dunowri oblong or square linings, thirty feet long and twenty feet deep, and subdivided into three or four compartments, were used.

When the stratum of soft soil is too thick for the foundations to be placed below it, the soil must be consolidated; or the area of the foundation must be sufficiently extended to enable the ground to support the load. The ground may be consolidated by wooden piles; but in soils where they are liable to decay, pillars of sand, or mortar, or concrete, rammed into holes previously bored, may be used. Artificial foundations are also formed by placing on the soft ground either a timber framework, surrounded occasionally by sheeting, or a mass of rubble stone, or a layer of concrete, or a thick layer of fine sand spread in layers eight to ten inches thick, which, owing to its semifluidity, equalizes the pressure. A remarkable example of this method was afforded in the restoration, in 1844, of the arched way at the Phillippeville gate, at Charleroi, where the old pile-work foundations had twice given way. A trench was dug $3\frac{1}{4}$ feet deep and $3\frac{1}{4}$ feet wider than the construction on each side, and inclosed by little walls. Into this cavity was put very fine sand, moderately wetted, then a layer of concrete, twenty inches thick, and upon this the masonry was built, which has stood perfectly. When the bottom of the excavation is silty, it is advisable to throw a thick layer of sand over it before driving piles, as the sand gives consistency to the silt.

A heavy superstructure is partially supported on a soft foundation by the upward pressure due to the depth below the surface to which it is carried, in the same manner that a solid floats in a liquid when it displaces a volume of water equivalent to its own weight. According to Rankine a building will be supported when the pressure at its base is $wh \left(\dfrac{1+\sin \psi}{1-\sin \psi}\right)^2$ per unit of area, where h is the depth of the foundation, w the weight of the soft ground per unit of volume, and ψ the angle of friction.

Mr. McAlpine, M. Inst. C.E., in building a high wall at Albany, U.S.A., succeeded in safely loading a wet clay soil with two tons on the square foot, but with a settlement depending on the depth of the excavation. In order to prevent a great influx of water, and consequent softening of the soil, he surrounded the excavation with a puddle trench, ten feet high and four feet wide, and he also spread a layer of course gravel on the bottom.

When the foundation is not homogeneous it is necessary to provide against unequal settlement, either by increasing the bearing surface where the ground is soft, or by carrying an arch over the worst portions.

HYDRAULIC FOUNDATIONS.

Under this head are comprised all foundations in rivers, and where running water has to be contended with.

Foundations are laid upon the natural surface where it is rocky, also on beds of gravel, sand, or stiff clay secured against scour by aprons, sheeting, rubble stones, or other means of protection. When the foundations are to be pumped dry, dams are resorted to if the depth of water is less than ten feet, and are specially applicable to the abutments of bridges, where the water is less deep and rapid and the bank forms one side of the dam. The dam can be made of clay, or even earth free from stones and roots, with slopes of 1 to 1; the width at the top being about equal to the depth of water when the depth does not exceed three feet in a current, or ten feet in still water. The leakage of a dam and the danger of breaches increase rapidly in proportion to the head of water. At Hollandsch Diep a great dam of sand, protected from the waves by fascines, had to keep out a head of water of twenty-three feet at high tides from the foundations. M. de la Gournerie constructed a temporary dam of silt, 4,265 feet long, at St. Nazaire, in 1849, to protect the shed of the floating dock. The dam was thirteen feet high, four feet wide at the top, with a pitched slope of 1 in 3 towards the sea, and an inner slope of 1 in 5.

Concrete makes a solid dam, but it is expensive to construct and difficult to remove. A masonry dam 328 feet long was built at Lorient in 1857.

A cofferdam with a double row of piles takes up less space and is less liable to be worn away or breached than an earthwork dam. At the Auray viaduct a dam was made of two rows of piles, with boards filling up the spaces between the piles, the center of the dam being filled with well-punned silt, and protected outside with rubble stones. It supported the pressure of a head of water of from five to eleven feet; its average cost was £1 0s. 10d. per lineal foot. The width of a cofferdam is often as great as the head of water; but if the cofferdam is strutted inside, so that the clay merely acts as a watertight lining, the width need not exceed from four to six feet. In a cofferdam of concrete at Marseilles constructed for the basin of the graving docks, the widths were calculated at 0.45 of the total height, the maximum width has thus attained twenty feet.

In building the viaduct of Lorient, on a foundation dry at low water, a single row of strutted piles, $3\frac{1}{4}$ feet apart, planked from top to bottom on both sides, was used (Fig. 6), and the space between the planking, ten inches wide, was filled with silt pressed down. When the filling is so much reduced in thickness the planks are carefully joined, and the

Fig. 6.

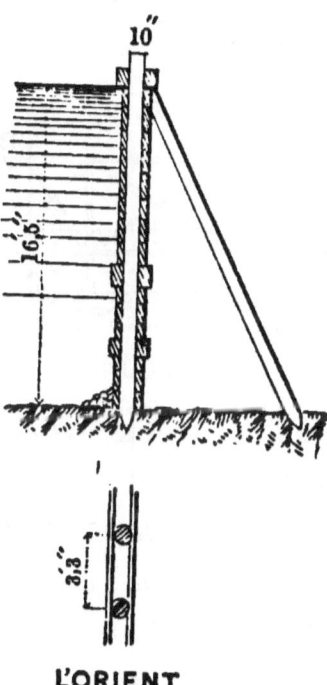

L'ORIENT

clay is mixed with moss or tow, or sometimes with fine gravel or pounded chalk. As water leaks through joints and connections, the ties are placed as high up as possible, and the bottom is scooped out or cleaned before the clay is put in. When the sides of the part to be inclosed are sufficiently close they may be effectually supported by a series of stays, as was done in making the dam for the construction of the apron of the Melun dam (Fig. 7), where struts were put in at intervals of 16½ feet.

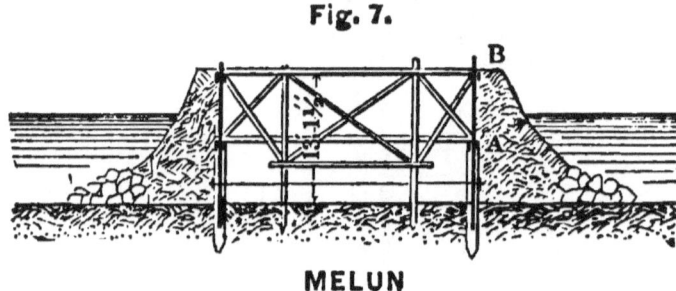

Fig. 7.

MELUN

The Grimsby Dock works, and the Thames Embankment works, furnished examples of cofferdams constructed to bear the pressure of a great head of water. For constructing the Zuider Zee locks on the Amsterdam Canal a circular dam, 525 feet in diameter, was erected, consisting of a double row of sheet piling, the piles being one foot square and fifty feet long, with walings attached. Eventually, in consequence of accidents, a third row was added, and the dam further strengthened by sloping banks of sand on both sides, the outer slope being protected by clay and fascine work. The head of water against the dam was occasionally twenty feet.

If large springs burst out in an excavation they must be either stopped up with clay or cement, or be confined within a wooden, brick, or iron pipe in which the water rises till the pressure is equalized, and then it is stopped up as soon as the masonry is sufficiently advanced and thoroughly set. If, however, there is a general leakage over the whole bottom of the excavation it must be stopped by a layer of concrete, incorporated with the foundation courses (Fig. 8).

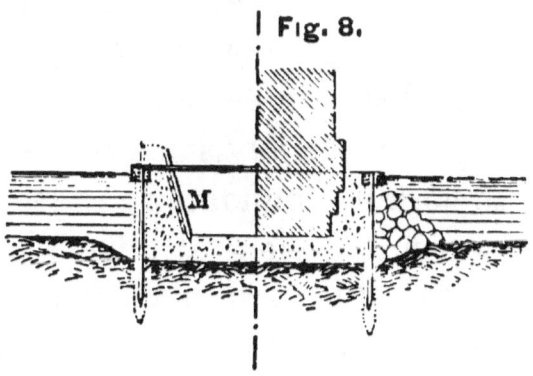

Fig. 8.

Cofferdams or troughs of concrete had been used on a large scale at Toulon and Algiers for the construction of repairing docks.

Where there is not space for a clay dam, timber sheeting well strutted and caulked is used. For instance at the Custom-house quay of Rio de Janeiro a dam of square sheet piling, with counterforts of cross sheet piling, and made watertight by hoop iron let into grooves in each pile, served to support the pressure of about twenty-three feet of water. A similar structure, however, at the West India Docks was floated away by an equinoctial spring tide, owing to the want of tenacity of the ground. When the head of water is under five feet, tarred canvas is sufficient to keep it out, the canvas being weighted at the bottom, and nailed to a beam at the top. It is in every instance advisable to take out the earthwork for foundations in lengths.

In the construction of the Victoria Docks a metallic cofferdam was used, which was very easily displaced by floating.

Hollow timber frames without a bottom, and made watertight at the bottom after being lowered by concrete or clay, are suitable in water from six to twenty feet deep on rocky beds, or where there is only a slight layer of silt. This method was resorted to by M. Beaudemoulin, between 1857 and 1861, at the St. Michael, Solferino, Change and Louis Philippe bridges at Paris. The timber frame at the St. Michael bridge was fifteen feet nine inches high, 125 feet long, and nineteen feet eight inches wide at the base, with a batter of 1 in 5; the uprights were six inches square, and $6\frac{1}{2}$ feet apart; the framework was made of oak, and the planks of deal (nine inches by three inches), the spaces between them being covered by small laths nailed on to the planks. Fourteen crabs placed on four boats supported the framing, and let it down as it was built up; this was weighted with stones to sink it on the foundations prepared by dredging, and the planks were then slipped between the walings and beaten down lightly. A toe of rubble stone outside supported the pressure of the concrete inside. The whole operation took ten days, and in one month the masonry was finished up to the plinth. The caisson, including erection, cost £560.

The caissons of the bridges at Vienna, sunk twelve feet below water level, cost £2 18s. 6d. per lineal yard of circumference. At the Point-du-Jour viaduct the caissons were 131 feet long, and from twenty-six to thirty-three feet wide, and from twenty-one to twenty-six feet high. The long sides were put together flat on the ground, and were lifted up to allow of the short sides being fixed to them. A few hours sufficed for depositing the caisson in its place. M. Picard in reconstructing the Bezons bridge, after the war of 1870, used caissons in two portions, as the lower portion had to remain, whilst the upper portion was only needed for a time. Some nails and straps fastened the two parts together. A layer of clay was placed under the rubble toe outside, to prevent leakage between the concrete and the planks. This expedient was first adopted by M. Desnoyers, in order to pump dry the foundation which he carried down into the clay, so as to build masonry walls on the bottom without using concrete. At the Aulne viaduct in Brittany, MM. Desnoyers and Arnoux made a caisson seventy-five feet six inches by thirty-four feet nine inches, and nearly twenty-three feet high (Fig. 9), and, with the excep-

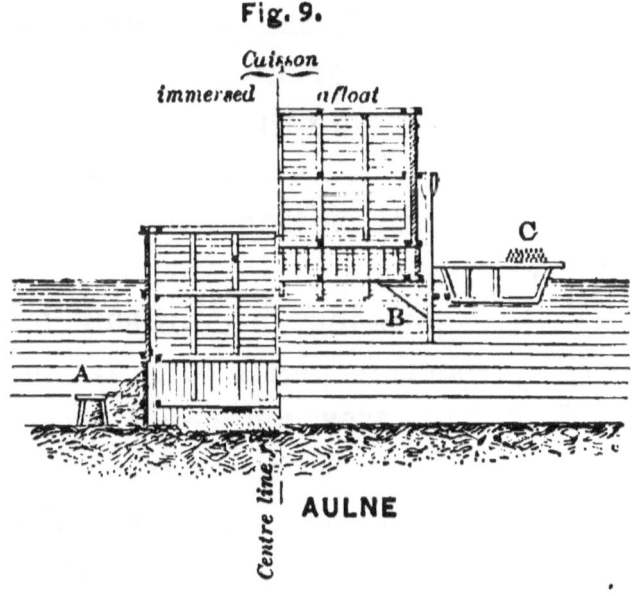

Fig. 9.

AULNE

tion of the bottom portion, caulked beforehand. When it was deposited the bottom planks were slid down between the lower set of walings, and a toe of puddled clay "A," protected from the rush of the current by canvas, was put round the bottom outside. The caisson was so watertight that a Letestu pump working two or three hours each day kept the foundations perfectly dry. When the caisson, put together on a stage supported on eight boats, was ready for depositing, the sluice doors of the Guily-Glas dam were opened, lowering the caisson till the projecting pieces "B" touched the ground, and by cutting the beams fastening these projections to the boats, the boats were set free. As the tide rose the caisson floated, and the boats were attached to its upper part, which, by lightening, lifted it sufficiently for the projecting pieces to be taken off. The depositing was completed by opening the sluices of the dam at high water, and as the water fell the caisson, weighted with rails, sank on the dredged bottom. Thus by the help of water alone a mass weighing seventy-four tons was safely and accurately deposited. The cost of one caisson was £740; and the cost of the foundation below low water did not exceed £1 12s. 6d. per cubic yard. At Lorient large caissons, from twenty-three to twenty-four feet high, were employed; but an interior dam of concrete forming a permanent part of the foundation was used instead of an external toe of clay. At Quimperlé M. Dubreil made the caisson watertight by a dam of clay inside, which necessitated a somewhat larger caisson, but admitted of the removal of the timber. When a limit to the space occupied is immaterial, as on the large American rivers, a sort of double-cased crib-work dam is frequently adopted. M. Malézieux has given various details of this class of work, such as the cofferdam in Lake Michigan to obtain the water supply for Chigaco. A caisson 200 feet long and 98 feet wide, inclosed by double watertight sides from thirteen to nineteen feet high, was used at Montreal on the St. Lawrence. The interval between the two sides was about eleven feet wide, and planked at the bottom so that the caisson could be floated into place. When the caisson was sunk, piles were driven in holes made in the bed of the river to keep it in place, and the bottom was made watertight by a lining at the sides of beams and clay. These kinds of caissons are only suitable where the bottom is carefully levelled. Although iron caissons are generally used for penetrating some distance into the soil, there are instances of iron caissons being merely deposited upon the natural bed. M. Pluyette founded one of the large piers at Nogent sur-Marne in a plate iron caisson, which weighed about seventy tons, and cost £3,600, with a bed of concrete in it ten feet thick and protected by rubble stone. Its dimensions at the bottom were seventy-two feet by 37¾ feet, with rounded corners and a batter of 1 in 15, 29½ feet high, including a length of five feet, which could be removed when the work was finished. The thickness of the plates was from ⅛ inch to ⅜ inch, and it was strutted inside with timber. The same system was adopted at Brême, where caissons sixty-nine feet by 16½ feet were used for the four ordinary piers, and the width increased to 42½ feet for the pier on which the bridge turns; their height was 11½ feet, and the thickness of the plates ⅜ inch. The operation of sinking the caissons from a floating stage occupied about seven hours. A layer of concrete nine feet thick was spread over the bottom and left for twelve weeks to set before the water was pumped out.

The methods employed for laying foundations in the water, either on the natural surface or after a slight amount of dredging, have next to be considered.

A rubble mound foundation is sometimes employed for dams where any settlement can be repaired by adding fresh material on the top; also for landing-piers in lakes by solidifying the upper portion with concrete, and in breakwaters where a masonry superstructure is erected on the top. Such a method, however, is not suitable where a slight settlement would be injurious; and in the sea the base of the mound is generally less exposed to scour than in a river.

Another method consists in sinking a framing, not made watertight, inside which concrete is run, and the framing remains as a protection for the concrete, and is surrounded by a toe of rubble. If the framing is of some depth iron tie-rods are put in by divers after the bottom has been dredged, to enable the framing to support the pressure of the concrete. When piles can be driven the framing is fixed to them. The piles, five to eight feet apart, have a double row of walings fixed to them, between which close planking is driven, from ten to fourteen inches wide, and from three to five inches thick, and sometimes, when the scour of a sandy subsoil has to be prevented, the planks are grooved and tongued, or have covering pieces put on by divers, or are driven in close panels. The insufficiency of a simple framing of planks for foundations on running sand was demonstrated by the destruction of the Arroux bridge at Digoin, and the Gue-Moucault bridge over the Somme by the flood of September 1866, in spite of the fascines and rubble stone protecting their piers, owing to the washing out of the underlying sand through small interstices by the rapid whirling current. The cost per superficial yard of a casing formed with piles and planks is about £1, including the cost of driving 6½ feet.

Open framing is sometimes used for inclosing a mound of rubble stone. These mounds require examination after floods, and renewing till the mound has become perfectly stable.

In permeable soils foundations of concrete inclosed in frames are frequently employed, as, for instance, for the foundations of the Saints Pères, Jena, Austerlitz, and Alma bridges at Paris; but in silty and watertight soils foundations in excavations pumped dry are preferable.

The bed of the Rhone at Tarascon, consisting of sand and gravel, in which piles are difficult to drive, is subject to scour in floods to a depth of 46 feet. Foundations, however, were laid there, at considerable expense, by frames with double linings, ten feet apart, in which large blocks were placed with unhewn stones on them; the ground was then dredged inside the frames to twenty-eight feet below low-water level, and 260 cubic yards of concrete were deposited in twenty-four hours.

Lastly, concrete can be deposited *in situ* for bridge foundations; and though concrete blocks are only used in sea works, bags of concrete, like those at Aberdeen, by Mr. Dyce Cay, M. Inst. C.E., might be sometimes employed, instead of rubble stones, for forming the base of piers or for preventing scour.

Piles are used where a considerable thickness of soft ground overlies a firm stratum, when the upper layer has sufficient consistency to afford a lateral support to the piles, otherwise masonry piers must be adopted.

The piles are usually placed from $2\frac{1}{4}$ to 5 feet apart, center to center, and the distance is occasionally increased to $6\frac{1}{2}$ feet for quays or other works only slightly loaded. Sometimes under abutments or retaining walls the piles are driven obliquely to follow the line of thrust. The Libourne bridge rests on piles $2\frac{1}{4}$ feet apart, and driven about forty feet in sand and silt. At the Voulzie viaduct, on the Paris and Mulhouse railway, some piles were driven eighty feet without reaching solid ground, and the ground between the piles had to be dredged, and replaced by a thick layer of concrete. Piles which have not reached firm ground sustain loads nevertheless, owing to the lateral friction, as, for instance, in the soft clay at La Rochelle and Rochefort piles can support 164 lbs. per square foot of lateral contact, and 123 lbs. in the silt at Lorient. On the Cornwall railway, viaducts were built upon piles, sixty-five to eighty feet long, driven, in groups of four fastened close together, by a four-ton monkey with a small fall. A timber grating is fastened to the top of the piles, or a layer of concrete is deposited, as at Dirschau, Hollandsch Diep, and Dordrecht; or both grating and concrete, as the grating distributes the load and strengthens the piles. Planking is sometimes put on the framing which distributes the pressure, as at London Bridge, but it is considered objectionable as it prevents any connection between the superstructure and the concrete, and increases the chance of sliding. The space between the piles from the river bed to low water is sometimes filled with rubble stones, and sometimes with concrete (Fig. 10), which is less liable to

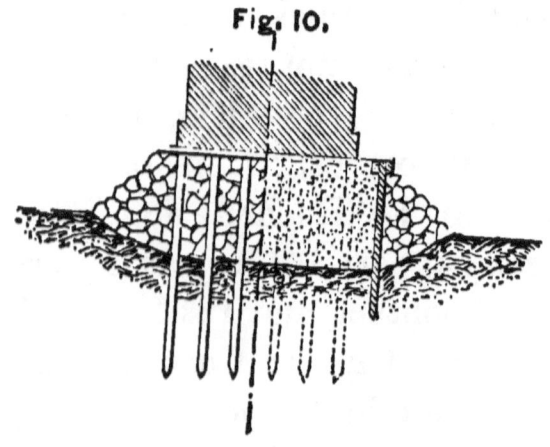

Fig. 10.

disturbance. When the ground is very soft a filling of clay has been preferred on account of its being lighter than concrete.

A mixed system of piling and water-tight caissons, of rubble filling and concrete, was adopted at the Vernon bridge. After the piles had been driven the spaces between them were filled up to half the depth of water with rubble stones: a caisson ten feet high was then placed on the top, and a bottom layer of concrete deposited in it. In a month's time the interior of the caisson was pumped dry, the heads of the piles cut off, and the filling with cement concrete completed to low-water level. The caisson was cut off to the level of the grating as soon as the pier was well above water. The foundation cost altogether £14 8s. per square yard of base of the pier.

The heavy ram of Nasmyth moved by steam, with a small fall, but giving sixty to eighty blows per minute, enabled piles to be driven thirty-three feet in a few minutes, and with much less chance of divergence or jumping than in driving with less powerful engines. In certain soils, in which there is a momentary resistance during pile-driving, it has been proposed to bore holes in which the pile should be afterwards driven.

At St. Louis the annular piles, $3\frac{1}{4}$ feet in diameter, made of eight pieces of wood, used for guiding the pneumatic caisson, were driven by the aid of the hydraulic sand-pump working inside, the invention of Mr. Eads, M. Inst. C.E.

The load that a pile driven home and secure from lateral flexion can bear may be estimated at from one-tenth to one-eighth of the crushing load, which varies between 5,700 and 8,500 lbs. per square inch. Thus, taking a fair load of 710 lbs. per square inch, a small pile of seven inches diameter will bear about twelve tons, and a pile of eighteen inches diameter will bear about eighty tons, and a pile to bear the load of twenty-five tons used as a unit by M. Perronet should be about ten inches in diameter. According to M. Perronet a pile can support a load of twenty-five tons as soon as it refuses to move more than $\frac{3}{8}$ inch under thirty blows of a monkey, weighing eleven cwts. ninety lbs., falling four feet or under ten blows of the same monkey falling twelve feet. At Neuilly, however, M. Perronet placed a load of fifty-one tons on piles thirteen inches square, but driving the pile till it refused to move more than $\frac{3}{16}$ inch under twenty-five blows of a monkey of the same weight falling 4½ feet; but such a load is unusual. At Bordeaux the driving was stopped when the pile did not go down more than $\frac{3}{16}$ inch under ten blows of a monkey, weighing 1,100 lbs., falling about fifteen feet, but one of the piers settled considerably, the load on a pile being twenty-two tons; whereas at Rouen, by insisting on M. Perronet's rule, no settlement occurred.

From experiments made at the Orleans viaduct, M. Sazilly concluded that piles might support with security a load of forty tons when they refuse to move more than $1\frac{2}{3}$ inch under ten blows of a monkey weighing fifteen cwts. and falling about thirteen feet.

Various formulæ have been framed for

calculating the safe load on piles, which are quoted in a paper by Mr. McAlpine, M. Inst. C.E., on "The Supporting Power of Piles," and in a Paper on "The Dordrecht Railway Bridge," by Sir John Alleyne, Bart., M. Inst. C.E. If Weisbach's formula is applied to M. Perronet's rule it appears that, assuming a safe load, the limiting set of the pile might be $3\frac{1}{4}$ inches instead of $\frac{3}{8}$ inch for ten blows; and the formula shows that large monkeys should be adopted in preference to a large fall, and in this it agrees with practice for preventing injury to the piles.

In order to provide against the danger of overturning in silty ground, the ground is sometimes first compressed by loading it with an embankment, which is cut away after a few months at those places where foundations are to be built. At the Oust bridge it was even necessary to connect the piers and abutments by a wooden apron, which, for additional security, was surrounded by concrete (Fig. 11). The abutment was made

Fig. II.

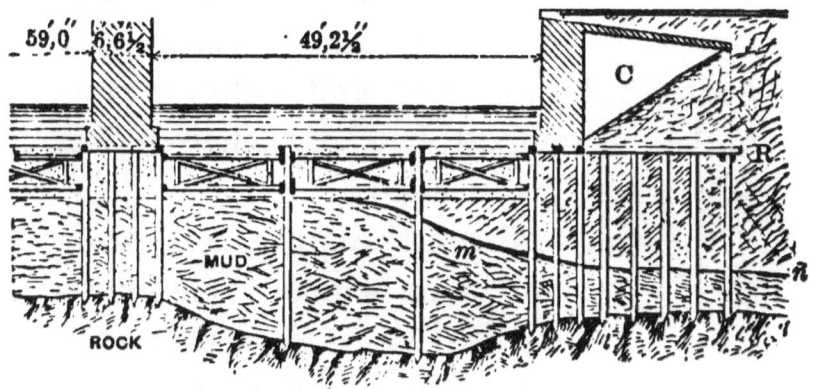

OUST VIADUCT

hollow to lighten it, and the embankment, "R," had compressed the silty ground to $m.n$. The foundations cost £23 1s. 7d. per superficial yard for depths of from thirty-three to forty-three feet from the natural surface to the rock, or £1 16s. 10d. per cubic yard, a high price due to the difficulties met with and the bad weather. At the bridge of Bouchemaine, near Angers, the bending of the piles, which traverse about twenty feet of silt, was stopped by surrounding them with great masses of rubble stones.

Occasionally foundations on piles have failed or suffered great sets or lateral displacements. At the Tours bridge, many arches have fallen at successive times; holes in the foundations had to be refilled with lime, and below certain arches a general bed of concrete was afterwards established.

Floating caissons require a bottom carefully levelled, on which to be lowered. Labelye, in 1750, deposited the caissons of old Westminster bridge on the dredged bottom of the river; but usually this kind of caisson is deposited on piles cut off to one level. These caissons have oak bottoms and movable sides of fir, and enable the masonry piers built inside to be lowered on piles previously driven. The oak bottom serves as a platform for the pier, and the movable fir sides can be used again for other caissons. At Ivry, with only two sets of movable sides, the contractor was able to put four caissons in place in one month. The bottom, which consists of a single or double platform, has timbers projecting underneath which fit on to the rows of piles. The movable sides are sometimes made in panels, which fit into grooves both in the bottom framing and in upright posts, placed about ten feet apart, which are tenoned at the bottom, and kept in place at the top by transoms going across the caisson. The different parts of the sides are tightly pressed together by the bolt, A B (Fig. 12). In other instances, as at the bridge

Fig 12.

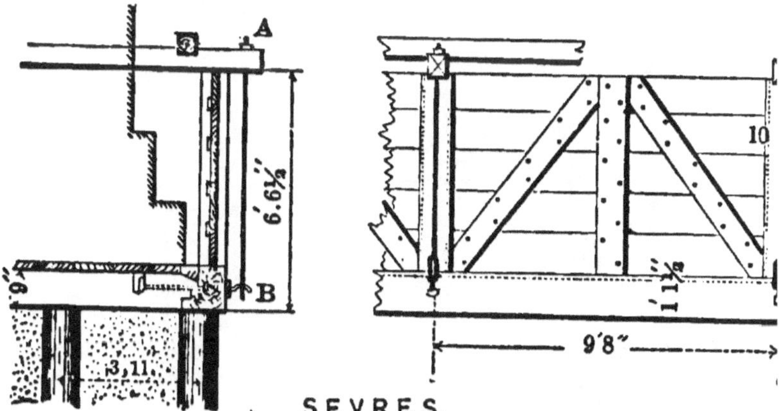

SEVRES.

of Val Benoit over the Meuse, the sides butt against the vertical sides of the bottom, against which they are pressed by keyed bolts, D, placed at intervals of five feet (Fig. 13). The caisson is kept near the shore whilst the first courses of masonry are being built in it; it is then, on a favorable opportunity, floated over the site of the pier prepared to receive it, and is gradually sunk by letting in water.

At the Bordeaux bridge the caissons had a height of twenty-six feet, and were divided in cases by transverse rods. This work, which comprises seventeen arches, was founded in a great depth of water, about the year 1820, by the engineers Deschamps and Billandel.

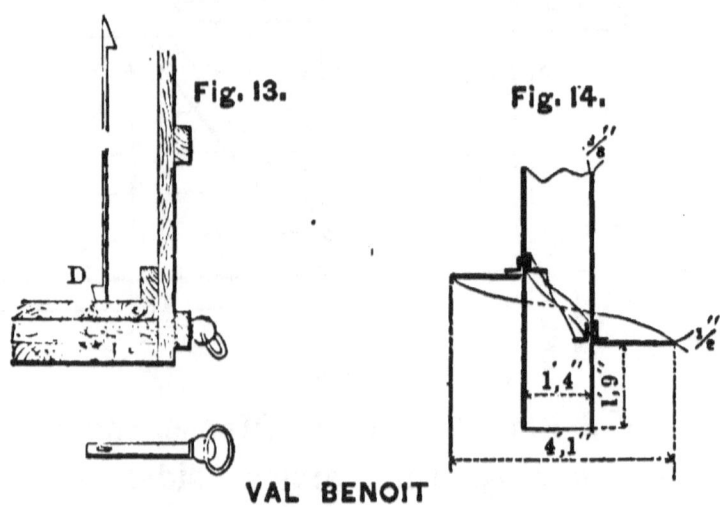

VAL BENOIT

In sea works the laying of foundations in the water is managed differently. Thus artificial blocks of concrete may be deposited by the help of divers, as at

Dover pier; or much larger masses may be moved by powerful machinery, as, for instance, blocks of 150 to 200 tons put down at Brest in 1868, and at Dublin by Mr. Stoney, M. Inst. C.E. For small landing piers, and for piers of bridges in rivers not exposed to the breaking up of ice, artificial blocks or metallic frameworks may be placed under water on the top of timber piles cut off level, a plan adopted by Mr. Maynard, M. Inst. C.E., on a foundation of screw piles.

Screw piles were introduced by Mr. Mitchell, M. Inst. C.E., for securing buoys. They can be applied with advantage to the construction of bollards and beacons, on account of the resistance they offer to drawing out; but as in the process of screwing down the ground is more or less loosened, judgment must be used in employing them for mooring or warping buoys. In foundations for beacons they should be screwed down from fifteen to twenty feet below the level to which the shifting sand is liable to be lowered. Even when all cohesion of the ground is destroyed in screwing down a pile, a conical mass, with its apex at the bottom of the pile and its base at the surface, would have to be lifted to draw the pile out. The resistance to settlement is also increased by the bearing surface of the screw; and the screw pile is accordingly to be preferred to an ordinary pile in soft strata of indefinite depth, or when the shocks produced by ordinary pile-driving are liable to produce a disturbance. The screw pile has likewise the advantage of being easily taken up.

Screw piles have been principally used in England and in the United States. They have usually one or two spirals projecting considerably from the shaft, these spirals being cylindrical for soft ground and conical for hard ground, and either of wrought iron or of cast iron. The shaft may be of wood or, by preference, of iron, which must be pointed at the end for hard ground, but cylindrical and hollow when the ground is soft. The screw will penetrate most soils except hard rock; it can get a short way into compact marl through loose pebbles and stones, and even enter coral reefs. A screw pile turned by eight capstan bars, twenty feet long, each moved by four or five men, with a screw four feet in diameter, passed in less than two hours through a stratum of sand and clay more than twenty feet thick, the surface of which was about twenty feet below water, and dug itself to a depth of about one foot into an underlying schistous rock. At the Clevedon pier screw piles penetrated hard red clay to depths varying between seven and seventeen feet, and although the screw had a pitch of five inches they rarely went down more than three inches in one turn. Mr. W. Lloyd, M. Inst. C.E., has recorded an unsuccessful use of screw piles, which in the shifting sandy bed of a South American river became twisted like a corkscrew, and were overturned in the first breaking up of the ice. At Hamburg screw piles, in sets of three and joined at the top, are used as bollards.

The piles are hollow wrought-iron tubes, ⅜ inch thick, furnished with a screw both inside and out, with a pitch of one foot (Fig. 14). To screw them down two capstans were used to pull the two ends of a rope wound round the head of the pile, the force transmitted to the pile being thirty times that applied at an arm of the capstan, and towards the close, when the pile had been forced down nearly thirteen feet, seven men were required to work each capstan. At the commencement each turn of the screw produced a descent of ten inches, and hardly nine inches at the end. A vessel struck, in 1852, against one of these bollards, and broke off the top without shifting the piles.

Piles with discs, used in the first instance at the Leven and Kent viaducts, by Mr. Brunlees, M. Inst. C.E., differ little from screw piles except in the method of sinking them. This operation was performed by sending a jet of water down a wrought-iron tube inside the cast-iron pile, which washed away the silty sand from underneath the disc and caused the pile to descend. The sinking cost about 2s. 6d. per lineal foot, whereas at Southport pier, where water was obtained from the waterworks, and ten piles were sunk per tide, the sinking only cost $4\frac{1}{2}$d. per lineal foot. Wooden piles, with a cast-iron shoe carrying a disc, might easily be sunk in the same manner, the water pipe being carried eccentrically through the disc.

Hollow wrought-iron piles have also been forced down by blows of a monkey, in silty and sandy ground interspersed with boulders, to a depth of about sixty feet; the thickness of the piles being about one-nine inch, and the diameter $19\frac{2}{3}$ inches. On the Cambrian railway, Mr. Conybeare, M. Inst. C.E., drove wooden piles down below the surface, by means of a lengthening piece of cast iron on the top, a piece of wood or lead being interposed between the monkey and the cast iron.

Large masonry piers carried through thick layers of soft ground to a solid bed may be constructed by various methods, and constitute the best kind of foundation in such a situation.

The method of cased wells is suitable where the silt is sufficiently compact and watertight to admit of pumping the well dry, and where the depth of water is small and can easily be kept out by a cofferdam or a caisson without a bottom. The well is sunk by the ordinary methods of sinking wells or driving headings in silty ground. At the Auray viaduct, a muddy stratum, twenty-six feet thick, was got through by this method. In building the abutment of a bridge over the Vilaine, in Brittany, resting on six pillars carried down fifty feet below the water-level, the same method was adopted; but for the lower portion of the excavation a smaller framing had to be sunk inside. A pillar fifty feet deep requires about twenty days for the excavation, and twelve days for building the masonry. The cost is from £1 16s. 10d. to £2 9s. per cubic yard of foundation complete. When the pier is so wide as to render the strutting difficult, an outer ring can be first lowered, which serves afterwards as a casing for excavating the inner portion. Where permeable gravel or very liquid silt has to be traversed it is necessary to resort to tubular foundations.

Cylindrical foundations are sunk with or without the aid of compressed air according to circumstances. These foundations possess the two great advantages of being capable of being sunk to a considerable depth, and of presenting the least obstruction to the current.

In a clay soil the cylinder acts as a movable cofferdam, which is sunk by being weighted, and enables the foundations inside to be built up easily and cheaply. This method was first adopted by Mr. Redman, M. Inst. C. E., at Gravesend; and afterwards at the Charing Cross and Cannon Street bridges; and also for the piers of the Victoria bridge over the Thames. Iron cylinders are preferred in certain cases to cylinders of brick, masonry, or concrete, on account of the ease with which they are lowered in deep water on to the river bed; in spite of the disadvantages attaching to them of high price, of the considerable weights required for sinking them, and lastly, of being only cases for the actual piers.

In 1823, Sir Mark Brunel, in sinking the wells of access to the Thames Tunnel used linings of brickwork, 50 feet in diameter, and resting on iron frames with vertical tie-rods. At Rochefort, M. Guillemain used linings of masonry resting on plate-iron rings and strengthened by iron chains; the wells were made sometimes 10 feet, sometimes 13 feet in diameter, and it was found that the facility and rate of descent of the larger linings more than compensated for the additional material. At Lorient the Caudan footbridge was built on four large rectangular frames, sunk from 50 to 60 feet below high water. When the ground is very soft it has a tendency to run into these tubular cofferdams when the water is pumped out.

The method of sinking wells in India has been previously referred to. Mr. Imrie Bell, M. Inst. C.E., added a pole to the jham used by the natives to save the trouble of diving, but even with this addition the process was slow. The foundations of the Poiney viaduct, on the Madras railway, were put in by this method. In more recent works the curb was made of iron instead of wood, and angular as in the case of the Jumna bridge. The first lengths were short, 5 to 6 feet, to insure a vertical descent; then a length of 10 feet, and afterwards lengths of 13 and 16 feet were added.

At the Glasgow bridge the lining was of cast-iron rings, being easier to lower in mid-stream; but for the quays and docks on the Clyde linings of brickwork and concrete were adopted for the sake of economy. Mr. Milroy, Assoc. Inst. C.E., considers that with concrete, which can be moulded to an edge at the bottom, all metal additions may be omitted where only silt or sand have to be traversed, and that the bottom ring should be of iron for penetrating harder soils. In the Clyde extension works the wells were filled up with concrete, and a double row of cylinders of 9 feet diameter were adopted in preference to a single row of 12 feet. It would be possible in this arrangement to take out the sand between the adjacent cylinders and form them into a solid mass by filling up these interstices with concrete. Mr. Ransome used cylinders of "apænite" for the Hermitage wharf on the Thames.

The Dutch engineers have often used oval-shaped iron tubes sunk by dredging inside. Thus in the bridge on the North Sea Canal the piers are elliptical; the one on which the opening portion turns having axes of 23 and 18 feet, and the others axes of $39\frac{1}{3}$ and 14 feet. The horizontal flanges and ribs were larger where the radius of curvature is increased, and the vertical ribs are not continuous, but arranged so as to overlap. The bridge over the Yssel, on the Utrecht and Cologne railway, rests upon cylinders which were sunk by internal dredging $17\frac{3}{4}$ feet below the river bed.

In France sinking cylinders by dredging is not often resorted to in rivers, possibly owing to a failure of this system at Perpignan, where the sinking of a masonry cylinder by dredging was stopped by boulders, and compressed air had to be used. However, the foundations of bridges at Rivesaltes, and over the Saône at Lyons, and the jetty made at Havre in 1861, were executed by this method. For the walls of the wet dock of Bordeaux rectangular wells have also been sunk by dredging.

The extension of the system must depend chiefly on improvements in the dredging machinery, of which the successive steps in advance already attained may be noted.

The jham was suspended by Kennard's sand pump. With this machine a well, $12\frac{1}{2}$ feet in diameter, was sunk in the Jumna 8 to 10 inches per hour by fourteen workmen. As the Kennard pump was not able to work in the compact clays and conglomerate met with in rebuilding the bridges over the Beas and the Sutlej

Bull's dredger was adopted, which consists of a semi-cylindrical case with jaws opening in two quadrants, like the American dredger of Morris and Cummings.

Mr. Stone, M. Inst. C.E., however, mentions that when it met with a hard stratum a descent of only 2 feet 10 inches was accomplished in three months, whereas in the upper layer the progress was much more rapid than with the sand-pump.

Next came Mr. Milroy's "excavator,' consisting of an octagonal frame from which are suspended eight triangular spades. These spades are forced vertically into the ground and are then lifted by chains so as to come together and inclose the earth, which can then be raised and discharged.

At the Glasgow bridge the progress was, on an average, $11\frac{1}{2}$ feet per day, and the maximum 20 feet. At Plantation Quay the average for a cylinder was about 4 feet per day, but these cylinders were impeded in their sinking by tongues and grooves, so that double this rate might be reckoned on for unconnected cylinders. Another machine is the "screw pan" used at the Loch Ken viaduct, a conical perforated vessel, the diameter at the top being 2 feet, and furnished at the bottom with a screw which enters the ground when turned.

The sand and mud entering the vessel are retained by little leather valves when the instrument is lifted. It works well in silt and clay; in harder soils a smaller vessel is needed.

Lastly there is the "boring head" used by Mr. Bradford Leslie, M. Inst. C.E., at the Gorai bridge. A revolving plane with blades underneath, able to disintegrate hard clays and compact sand, is worked inside the cylinder, and at the same time the excavated material is drawn up and removed from the cylinder by a siphon. To maintain an upward pressure in the siphon the level of the water in the cylinder is always kept higher than in the river. The boring-head made one revolution in about one minute and a half or two minutes, and excavated through clayey and sandy silt at a rate of about 1 foot per hour. One advantage possessed by this system is that the rate of progress is independent of the depth. The side piers of the Gorai bridge were sunk 124 feet below the surface, and the river piers 98 feet below low-water level. The only bridge the foundations of which have been carried down as deep as those of the Gorai bridge is the St. Louis bridge over the Mississippi; but the method of compressed air used in this work, looking at the difficulties and loss of life attending it, would have been impracticable with coolie labor at Gorai. The system of sinking by dredging is generally to be preferred to the compressed air system, except where numerous obstacles, such as boulders or embedded trees, are met with.

The friction between cylinders and the soil depends on the nature of the soil and the depth of sinking. For cast iron sliding through gravel the co-efficient of friction is between 2 and 3 tons on the square yard for small depths, and reaches 4 or 5 tons where the depth is between 20 and 30 feet. In certain adhesive soils it would be more. In sinking the brick and concrete cylinders in the silt of the Clyde it was found to amount to about $3\frac{1}{2}$ tons per square yard.

Passing on to the consideration of the pneumatic systems, the process of Dr. Potts was one of the first employed for sinking tubular foundations by the help of air. The cylinder in process of being sunk was connected with a vessel in which a vacuum was produced, and a communication between them being suddenly made a shock was produced by the rush of air. By this means Mr. Cowper, M. Inst. C.E., succeeded in driving down cylinders 5 feet at a time. The only novelty in the system was using air for applying a downward pressure on the cylinder, as dredging had still to be resorted to for removing the earth from the inside, and, moreover, there was a considerable influx of the surrounding soil, and frequent divergencies from the perpendicular. Mr. Bramwell, M. Inst. C.E., observing the effects produced by the rush of air out of the cylinder, in an aqueous soil, suggested sinking by forcing water from the interior of the cylinder towards its external surface, a process which would disintegrate the earth lubricate the sliding cylinder, and prevent the influx of the soil. The difficulties of the Potts process increase with the size of the cylinder; and for sinking the cylinders, 10 feet in diameter, of the Shannon bridge it was abandoned after an unsuccessful attempt.

The method of compressed air for enabling operations to be conducted under water is merely a modification of the diving-bell; but the application of it to a cylinder forced down by undermining was first made, in 1839, at Chalons for working a coal seam rendered inaccessible by the infiltrations of the Loire. After having begun the shaft by beating down a cylindrical lining of sheet iron, $3\frac{3}{8}$ feet in diameter, it occurred to the engineer, M. Triger, to cover over the top of the cylinder, and by forcing air in to drive out the water and admit the workmen. An air chamber was formed at the top with double doors, serving as a sort of lock for the passage in and out of the cylinder of men and materials without giving an outlet to the compressed air, and a pipe running up the cylinder carried off the water from the bottom. In 1845 M. Triger sank another cylinder, 6 feet in diameter, in the same way, and suggested the employment of the method for the foundations of bridges.

The first bridge foundations of this kind were carried out, in the years 1851-52, at the Rochester bridge on the Medway, which has masonry piers each supported on fourteen cylinders, 6 feet 11 inches in diameter, filled with concrete. Having begun with the Potts process till on alighting on old foundations it proved useless, Mr. Hughes, M. Inst. C.E., conceived the notion of reversing the current of air, and sinking the cylinders by the help of compressed air. The success of this method recalled to mind earlier suggestions in the same direction, such as the patent of Lord Cochrane, in 1830, for excavating foundations by compressed air, and the suggestion of M. Colladon of Geneva to Sir M. Brunel to try to stop the rush of water into the Thames Tunnel by forcing in air.

At the Chepstow bridge foundations the late Mr. I. K. Brunel, Vice-President Inst. C.E., abandoned the Potts process on coming upon an embedded tree, and resorted to compressed air, which he also subsequently employed in commencing the foundations of the iron cofferdams used for the piers of the Saltash bridge.

The various details of the compressed air system are given in the descriptions of the works in which it has been employed. Theoretically, when the lower edge of the cylinder has reached a depth of h feet below the surface of the water, the pressure required for driving the water out of the excavations is $\frac{3.14}{h}$ atmospheres; but frequently the intervention of the ground between the bottom of the river and the excavation enables the work to be carried on at a less pressure, as Mr. Brunel did at Saltash. A considerably greater pressure would be required if the water had to be forced from the excavation through the soil below the river bed; but this is avoided by placing a pipe inside to convey away the water, and M. Triger has found that the lifting of the water was facilitated by the introduction of bubbles of air into the pipe at a certain height.

Pressures of 2 or even up to 3 atmospheres do not injure healthy and sober men, and suit best men of a lymphatic temperament, but prove injurious to men who are plethoric or have heart disease. It is advisable to avoid working in hot weather, and each workman should not work more than four hours per day, or more than six weeks consecutively. At Harlem, New York, however, workmen have remained ten hours under a pressure of 50 feet, and even 80 feet of water. On the other hand, at St. Louis under a pressure of little more than 3 atmospheres several men were paralyzed or died, and the period of work was gradually reduced from four hours to one hour. From experiments on animals M. Bart has found that the accidents caused by a sudden removal of pressure are due to the escape of the excess of gas absorbed by the blood. Beyond 6 atmospheres any sudden return to the normal pressure is attended with danger; the usual rule now is to allow one minute per atmosphere. The cylinders subjected to pressure should be furnished with safety valves, pressure gauges, and alarm whistles, as explosions occasionally occur.

Iron rings from 6 feet to 13 feet in diameter are cast in one piece, and a caoutchouc washer is introduced at the joints between the rings; cylinders of larger diameter are cast in segments, and cylinders of smaller diameter than 6 feet are rarely used. The thickness is usually $1\frac{1}{8}$ inch, increased to $1\frac{1}{2}$ inch or $1\frac{7}{8}$ inch were exposed to blows, in conical joining lengths, and in the bottom length.

When two cylinders have to be sunk close together it is best to sink them alternately, as they tend to come together when sunk at the same time. At Macon, where there was only an interval of $3\frac{1}{4}$ feet between two cylinders, one of the cylinders was seen to rise suddenly as much as 6 feet when the other was forced down. Sometimes where cylinders of small diameter have to be used the excavations are extended beyond the cylinder at the bottom, and filled with concrete to give a greater bearing surface; this plan was adopted at Harlem bridge, New York, and by the late Mr. Cubitt, Vice-President Inst. C.E., at the Blackfriars railway bridge. Another way of accomplishing the same object is by enlarging the lower rings of the cylinder, and putting in a connecting conical length, as was done by Sir John Hawkshaw, Past-President Inst. C.E., at the Charing Cross and Cannon Street bridges.

The cylinders at Bordeaux were forced down by MM. Nepveu and Eiffel, in 1859–60, by strong beams of wrought iron, moved up or down by the pistons of four hydraulic presses, having 11 feet length of stroke and exerting a pressure of 60 to 70 tons; the force could be applied at pleasure, and regulated according to circumstances. At Argenteuil, where cylinders 12 feet in diameter had to be sunk, the concreting inside was carried on during the sinking, leaving only a circular shaft in the center, 3 feet 7 inches in diameter, lined with wooden framing, and enlarged at the bottom to a conical shape by a sort of cage of inclined beams butting against the bottom of the shaft (Fig. 18). The cylinders were sunk 50 feet on the average below low-water level, through mud, sand, gravel, and clay, on to marl or limestone, and four screw-jacks of 20 tons power supported the bottom ring by means of flat iron straps. After the sinking was completed the chamber at the bottom was filled with cement concrete, poured around iron pipes placed near the sides so as to maintain the pressure of air during the operation. When this layer of concrete was set the pipes were closed with cement, the normal pressure restored, and the shaft filled up with concrete. Concrete deposited under compressed air appears to set quicker, and to increase somewhat in strength, provided it is deposited in thin layers allowing the excess of water to escape. At Szègedin this was effected by mixing very dry bricks with the concrete. At Perpignan the foundations of a bridge over the Tet had been commenced by sinking a masonry cylinder by dredging inside, but large stones being unexpectedly met with the method of compressed air had to be resorted to. The masonry cylinder, $3\frac{1}{4}$ feet thick and 13 feet outside diameter, with a batter outwards of 1 in 100, was lined inside with neat cement, and was covered with a plate-iron top $\frac{1}{8}$ inch thick. The sinking was assisted when necessary by letting out air; the depth attained was about 26 feet. The cylinder was filled with concrete, which for the first 6½ feet was deposited under pressure. The success attending this experiment has led M. Basterot to recommend the deliberate application of compressed air to masonry cylinders for depths of less than 33 feet below water, and he estimates the cost of such a cylinder, 13 feet in diameter, sunk by this method 26 feet deep and filled in, at £340.

The foundations of the piers of the Kehl bridge were accomplished by the engineers, MM. Fleur Saint-Denis and Vuigner, by a combination of the principles of the compressed air process, the sinking of a pier by its own weight, the sinking by dredging, and the cofferdam system. As the bed of the Rhine at Kehl consists of large masses of gravel liable to be disturbed to a depth of 55 feet below low-water level, it was deemed advisable to carry the foundations down about 70 feet below low water. For the two central piers the chamber of excavation was divided into three caissons, the length of each being 18 feet 4 inches, the width of the foundation. For the piers forming the abutments for the swing bridges there were four caissons, each 23 feet long, the breadth of all the caissons being 19 feet. The plate iron forming the caissons was $\frac{3}{8}$ inch thick at the top, and $\frac{5}{16}$ inch thick at the sides, and strengthened by flanges and gussets. The top was strengthened by double T beams for supporting the weight of the masonry above. There were three shafts to each caisson, two being air shafts, $3\frac{1}{4}$ feet in diameter, one being in use whilst the other was being lengthened or repaired; the other shaft in the center was oval, open at the top and dipping into the water in the foundations at the bottom, so that the water could rise in it to the level of the river. In this shaft a vertical dredger with buckets was always working, and the laborers had only to dig, to regulate the work, and remove any obstacles. The screw-jacks controlling the rate of descent had a power of 15 tons, and were in four pairs. The wooden framing serving as a cofferdam was erected above the chamber of excavation; it was useful at the commencement for getting below the water, but might subsequently have been dispensed with. It was also found by experience that the caissons were sunk better in one division than in several divisions, and doors of communication were accordingly made through the double partitions. The iron linings to the air shafts were removed before the shaft was filled up. The shaft containing the dredger was at first made of iron, but afterwards of brick for the sake of economy. The sinking occupied sixty-eight days for one abutment, and thirty-two days for the other, giving a daily rate of 1 foot 1 inch and 1 foot $8\frac{1}{2}$ inches respectively. The sinking of the caissons for the intermediate piers took twenty to thirty days, which gives a daily rate of two feet $7\frac{1}{2}$ inches (Fig. 15).

For large works, where the load on the foundations is considerable, carrying

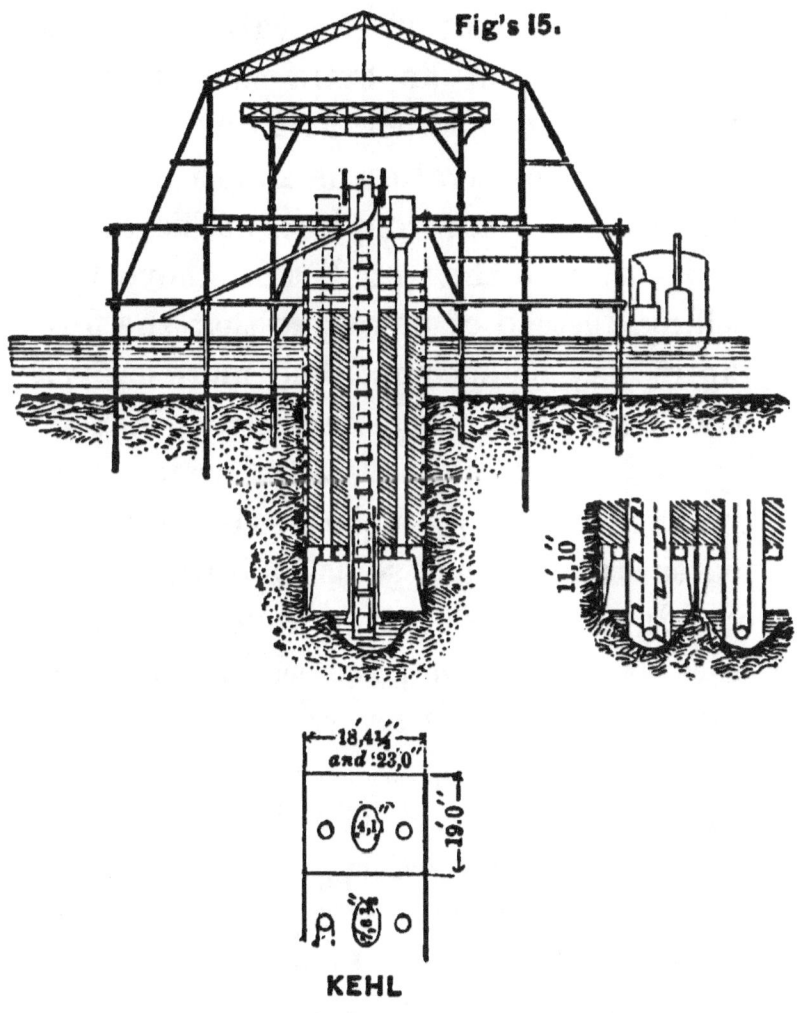

Fig's 15.

KEHL

down the foundations to a hard bottom is much better than piling. The dredger used at Kehl cannot be regarded as universally applicable. Some soils are not suitable for dredging, and in other cases the small amount of excavation renders the addition of an extra shaft inexpedient, as for instance at Lorient. The chamber of excavation is almost invariably made of plate iron, but, unlike those at Kehl, with the iron beams above the ceiling, instead of below, so that the filling in may be accomplished more easily. The cutting edge is always strengthened by additional plates. At Lorient the thickness was $2\frac{3}{16}$ inches, with several plates stepped back so as to form a sort of edge; the sides were about $\frac{1}{2}$ inch thick at the bottom, and $\frac{5}{16}$ inch at the top, and the roof was curved a little to increase its strength. At Vichy the plates were about $\frac{1}{4}$ inch thick. At La Voulta, Hollandsch Diep, and Lucerne, a sort of masonry lining was placed against the iron plates, and kept in place by gusset plates, to afford greater rigidity against the pressure of the earth. At St. Maurice wooden struts were substituted for angle-iron flanges; and at Vichy struts were put in at the base of the caisson, and also half-way up to support the sides. In consequence of these modifications, the caisson at Lucerne ($55\frac{3}{4}$ feet by $13\frac{3}{4}$ feet) weighed only 28 tons; the caisson at St. Maurice ($32\frac{3}{4}$ feet by $14\frac{1}{2}$ feet) weighed 14 tons; whereas at Kehl, a caisson, 23 feet by 19 feet, weighed 34 tons; at Lorient ($39\frac{1}{3}$ feet by $11\frac{1}{2}$ feet) weighed $27\frac{1}{2}$ tons; and at Riga ($64\frac{1}{3}$ feet by 16 feet) weighed $45\frac{3}{4}$ tons. The height of the chamber of excavation should be about 8 feet 10 inches. Frequently the cofferdam casing is of iron, as at Kehl, which protects the newly-built masonry from friction; and the upper portion of the casing can be removed when the work is completed. In a sea bed, with a silty bottom, special precautions must be taken against overturning, as variations in weight, according to the depth of immersion, are added to the effects of the current. Some divergence from the perpendicular at Lorient was due partly to this cause, but partly also to the absence of supporting screw-jacks. At Lorient there were two air locks, each connected with two shafts, in which balanced skips went up and down (Fig. 16). On the top of the bot-

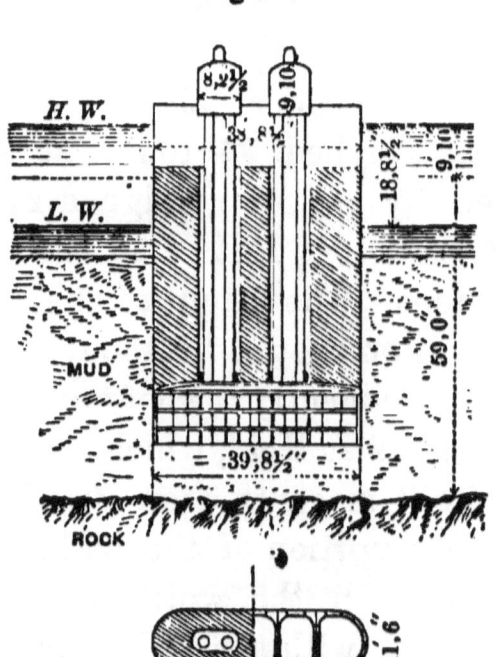

Fig's 16.

tom caisson a casing of sheet iron, from $\frac{3}{16}$ to $\frac{1}{8}$ inch thick, and weighing about 15 tons, was erected in successive rings. At the Nantes bridges, built in 1863 by M. M. Gouin for the railway of Roche-sur-Yon, twenty-two caissons were erected, and the depth of the concrete foundations varied from 39 to 62 feet. The same firm were the contractors for the pneumatic foundations at Hollandsch Diep for three piers, two being carried about 80 feet below high-water level, and the other 65 feet. As the river bed was very soft down to 50 feet below high water, and injury from storms might be apprehended, it was necessary to perform the first part of the sinking as rapidly as possible. The working chambers, and the lower 16 feet of the caisson, and the shafts for 23 feet in height, were erected on the bank, and masonry built on the horizontal projections of the chambers. Each caisson was then slid down an inclined plane to low-water mark, and at high water two boats fastened together removed them to their proper site, where they were deposited and gradually sunk into the ground. The excavation, the building up of the masonry, and the addition of successive lengths to the caisson, were carried on simultaneously. As the earthwork was easily removed, the caissons sank at a rate of from $1\frac{1}{2}$ foot to $3\frac{1}{4}$ feet per day. The first two piers were each completed in forty-five days from the launching of the caissons.

The Americans have adopted the pneumatic system for some large works, and introduced improvements. At the St. Louis bridge the foundations were carried to a greater depth than had ever been previously attained; and at East River bridge compressed air was used in wooden caissons of large dimensions. The particulars of the St. Louis bridge have been given by Mr. Francis Fox, M. Inst. C.E. The hydraulic sand pumping tube of Mr. Eads must only be recorded. The following details of the East River bridge are derived from the treatise of M. Malézieux, previously referred to. The Brooklyn pier was to be carried 50 feet and the New York pier 75 feet below high water. To provide against unequal sinking, owing to the variable nature of the soil, consisting of stiff clay mixed with blocks of trap rock, Mr. Roebling decided to place the bottom of the piers upon a thick platform of timber which formed the roof of the working chamber (Fig. 17). The sides were also

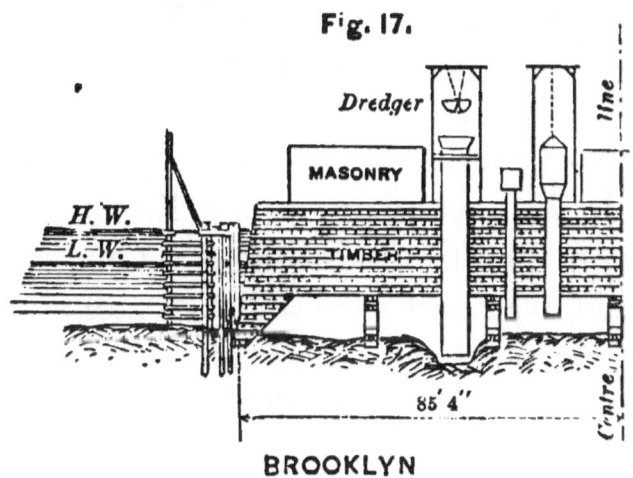

Fig. 17.

BROOKLYN

made of wood, as being easier than iron to launch and deposit on the exact site. The roof consisted of five tiers of beams, 1 foot deep, of yellow pine, placed one above the other and crossed, the beams being tightly connected by long bolts. The working chamber was 167 feet by 102 feet, and 10 feet clear height. The side walls had a V section, with a cast-iron edge covered with sheet iron; the walls had a batter inside outwards of 1 to 1, and 1 in 10 on the outside. Five transverse wooden partitions, 2 feet thick at the bottom, served to regulate the sinking. When the caisson had been put in place, twelve tiers of beams were added on the roof of the chamber of the Brooklyn pier, and nineteen on that of the New York pier, so that the top rose above water, and the masonry could be built without a cofferdam lining. The excavation, to the extent of 19,600 cubic yards, was performed in five months by Morris & Cumming's scoop dredger, working in two large shafts, dipping into the water at the bottom, and open above. When hard soil was met with these shafts were shut, and the excavation performed by manual labor under compressed air. In the New York caisson the total number of shafts was nine. The blocks of trap rock impeded the progress considerably; they had to be discovered by boring, and shifted or broken before the caisson reached them. When under 26 feet of water they could be blown up; this enabled the rate of progress, which had been 6 inches per week, to be doubled or trebled. When the caisson had reached a compact soil, it was possible to reduce the pressure to two-thirds of an atmosphere in excess of the normal pressure, and water had occasionally to be poured into the open shafts to maintain the proper water-level in them. By frequent renewal of the air, a supply was furnished for one hundred and twenty men and for the lights; and the temperature was kept nearly constant throughout the year at 86° within the caisson, whilst in the open air it varied from 10S° to 0°. As the load increased as the caisson went down, the roof of the Brooklyn caisson was eventually supported by seventy-two brick piers, so that the caisson might not become deeply embedded in the event of a sudden escape of air. In the New York caisson two longitudinal partitions were added, which served the same purpose.

In the silty sand which was frequently met with, a discharge pipe, up which the sand was forced by compressed air, proved very useful, discharging a cubic yard in about two minutes. The New York caisson (170 feet by 102 feet) was sunk in five months; the earthwork removed amounted to 26,000 cubic yards. The cheapness of wood in America permits a much freer use of it there than could be attempted in Europe.

When the watertight nature of the lower soil in the foundations of the East River bridge is considered, coupled with the inconveniences experienced in working under compressed air, as shown at the St. Louis bridge, it seems probable that in some future large work it may be possible to commence sinking a large caisson with compressed air, and after a better stratum is reached open all the shafts. The operation could then be completed by pumping out the small amount of water that might come in, and excavating in the ordinary way, as is often done in England, on a small scale, where the excavation to sink the cylinders to a water-tight stratum is performed by divers. If, as M. Morandière suggests, the air-lock was placed close over the working chamber, or even inside it, which would save constant alterations and allow of its being of larger dimensions, it would be desirable to have a special air-lock at the top, so that in the event of an accident the men might run up the shaft without the delay occasioned by passing through the air-lock. At Bordeaux the air-lock was formed by fixing one circular plate at the top and another at the bottom of one of the rings of the cast-iron cylinder, so that it was unnecessary to remove it each time that an additional ring was added. To save loss of air the air-lock should be opened very seldom, or made very small if required to be opened often. At Argenteuil the air-lock had an annular form (Fig. 18) with two compartments C, C', each having an external and an internal door. One compartment was put in communication with the interior to be filled with the excavated material, whilst the other was being emptied by the outer door, so that the loss of air was diminished without any

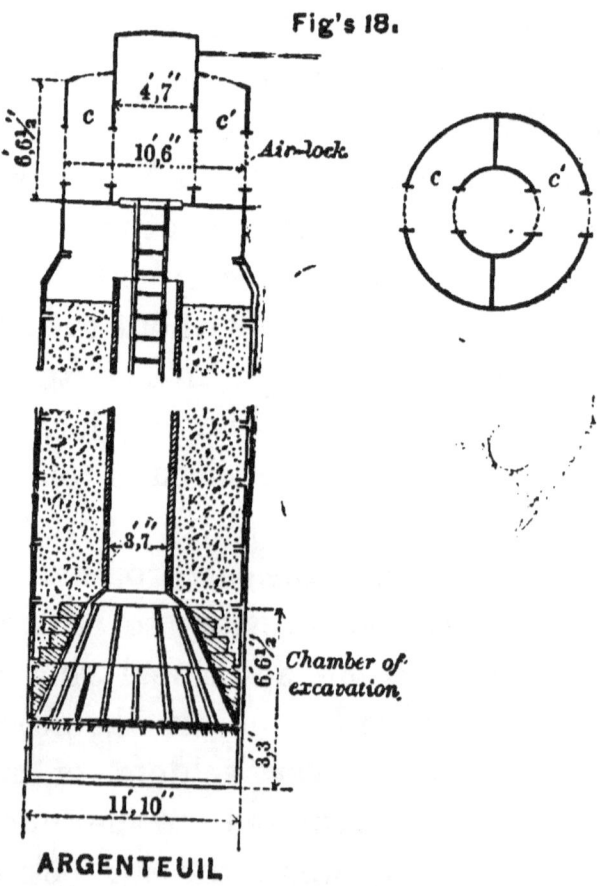

Fig's 18.

ARGENTEUIL

interruption to the work. Sometimes a double air-lock with one large and one small compartment is used; the large one being only opened to let gangs of workmen pass, and the small one just big enough to admit a skip and to contain a little crane for moving it. By having a small air-lock opened frequently, any sudden alterations in pressure are diminished. A more complete arrangement was adopted at Nantes (Fig. 20). There a sheet-iron cylinder was placed on the top of the double shaft in which the skips worked, having at one side a crescent-shaped chamber, a, serving to pass four men, and also on either side two concrete receivers, d, d', having doors above and below. There was also a shoot below for turning the concrete into the foundations, and a box, b, c, holding a little wagon which emerges at c after having been filled from an upper door, b. This last contrivance resembles that devised at Vichy by M. Moreaux (Fig. 19). The cast-iron box L, N, going

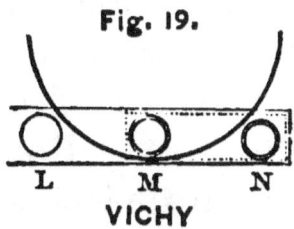

Fig. 19.

VICHY

across a segment of the air chamber, has three orifices, L, M, N, and a drawer with two compartments slides inside it. If these compartments are at M and N, the left one at M is filled whilst the other at N is emptied. Then by a rack movement the drawer is pushed back till

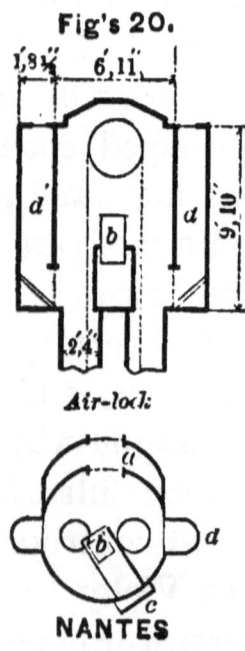

Fig's 20.

Air-lock.

NANTES

the compartment to the right comes to the center of the box, that is to say, into the air-lock, and the other is emptied outside at L. At Rotterdam, M. Michaëlis put a little inclined trough at the bottom of the principal air-lock, and closed it at each extremity by a valve, so that it both formed a little independent air-lock and also a shoot for the excavation. Mr. Smith employed the same system at the Omaha bridge over the Missouri. By not permitting the earthwork to enter the principal air-lock, it was possible to keep six great glazed bull's-eyes clean, by which both the daylight was admitted and at night the light was thrown from a reflector. The use of lamps inside, smoking and giving a bad light, was thus dispensed with.

The Author next proposes to give some details of the cost of foundations constructed by the help of compressed air. At Moulins cast-iron cylinders, 8 feet 2½ inches in diameter, with a filling of concrete and sunk 33 feet below water into marl, cost £12 18s. 6d. per lineal foot, or £6 2s. for the ironwork, and £6 16s. 6d. for sinking and concrete. At Argenteuil, with cylinders 11 feet 10 inches in diameter, the sinking alone cost £8 13s. 2d. per lineal foot, and one cylinder was sunk 53½ feet in three hundred and ninety hours; and at Orival, £7 12s. 5d., where the cylinder was sunk 49 feet in twenty days. At Bordeaux, with the same sized cylinders, a gang of eight men conducted the sinking of one cylinder, and usually 34 cubic yards were excavated every twenty-four hours. The greatest depth reached was $55\tfrac{3}{4}$ feet below the ground, and 71 feet below high water. In the regular course of working, a cylinder was sunk in from nine to fifteen days, and the whole operation, including preparations and filling with concrete, occupied on the average twenty-five days. One cylinder, or a half pier, cost on the average £2,320, of which £300 was for sinking. M. Morandière estimates the total cost of a cylinder sunk like those at Argenteuil, at a depth of 50 feet, at £1,440.

Considering next the cost of piers of masonry on wrought-iron caissons of excavation; the foundations of the Lorient viaduct over the Scorff cost the large sum of £4 19s. per cubic yard, owing to difficulties caused by the tides, the labor of removing the boulders from underneath the caisson, and the large cost of plant for only two piers. The foundations of the Kehl bridge cost still more, about £5 16s. per cubic yard; but this cannot be regarded as a fair instance, being the first attempt of the kind.

The foundations of the Nantes bridges, sunk 56 feet below low-water level, cost about £3 1s. per cubic yard. The average cost per pier was as follows:

	£
Caisson (41 feet 4 inches by 14 feet 5 inches), 50 tons of wrought-iron at £24	1,200
Cofferdam, 3 tons of wrought-iron at £12	36
Excavation, 916 cubic yards at 18s. 4d.	840
Concrete	860
Masonry, plant, &c.	384
	£3,320

One pier of the bridge over the Meuse at Rotterdam, with a caisson of 222 tons and a cofferdam casing of 94 tons, and sunk 75 feet below high water, cost £14,550, or £2 17s. 5d. per cubic yard.

The Vichy bridge has five piers built on caissons, 34 feet by 13 feet, and the abutments on caissons 26 feet by 24 feet. The foundations were sunk 23 feet in the ground, the upper portion consisting of shingle and conglomerated gravel, and the last 10 feet of marl. The cost of the bridge was as follows:

	£
Interest for eight months and depreciation of plant worth £4,000.............	800
Cost of preparations, approach bridge and staging........................	1,007
Caissons, No. 7, 150¾ tons at £23 6s.....	3,513
Sinking...............................	2,017
Concrete and masonry.................	1,089
Contractor's bonus and general expenses	1,254
	£9,680

The cost per cubic yard of foundation below low water was £3 8s. 7d., of which the sinking alone cost 15s. 3d. in gravel, and 19s. in marl. At St. Maurice the cost per cubic yard of foundation was £3 5s. 6d., exclusive of staging.

The Author has treated of the subject of tubular foundations at some length, because they are the most effectual means at the disposal of engineers for carrying foundations to great depths below water. Economical considerations render it desirable to adopt pumping or dredging when possible; but compressed air is very serviceable where boulders or other obstacles are met with, or where, as at Vichy, the ground is conglomerated and unsuitable for dredging. In cases where the proper course to be adopted is a matter of doubt, the success at the Gorai bridge, and the power of resorting to the aid of divers, if necessary, would encourage an attempt being made to dispense with compressed air, which at great depths, such as 100 feet under water, is attended with danger. The Tet bridge, moreover, furnishes an example of the possibility of resorting at last to compressed air if found indispensable.

In soft ground of unknown depth the best methods for making foundations are those already described; but it is sometimes advisable in small works to adopt more economical methods. Two distinct cases have to be considered :—
1. Where the soil is firm, but liable to be scoured to great depths; 2. Where the soil is soft as well as exposed to considerable scour.

Régemortes gained a reputation by

his method of dealing with an instance of the first of these two cases at Moulins, where several bridges had been destroyed one after another by scour in floods, owing to the piles on which they rested being unable to penetrate far enough into the film sand composing the bed of the Allier.

Régemortes, in 1750, renounced the idea of finding a stable foundation far down, and built on the surface, rendering it secure from scour by covering it with a masonry apron. The apron, having a uniform thickness of 6 feet (Fig. 21),

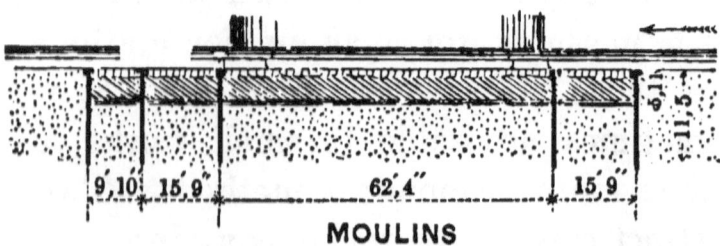

Fig. 21.

MOULINS

was laid on the dredged and levelled bed, dried by diverting the stream, or, in some places, by inclosing it with timber and pumping out the water. The infiltration through the bottom was stopped by depositing a layer of clay all over, and then lowering caulked timber panels in it. This method has, however, been much simplified by the introduction of hydraulic concrete. The apron at the West Viaduct at Amsterdam consists of a layer of concrete, 4 feet thick, placed on piling, and protected at the ends by sheeting. The apron of the Guétin canal bridge, constructed by M. Jullien in 1829, is 69 feet wide, 5 feet 5 inches thick, and 1,640 feet long. The concrete was carried down to a depth of $11\frac{1}{2}$ feet at each end between two rows of sheeting $6\frac{1}{2}$ feet apart. Another form of apron was adopted at the Ain bridge (Fig. 22), with a single row of sheeting at each end, $26\frac{1}{4}$ feet from the facing of the bridge at the lower end, and $11\frac{1}{2}$ feet at the upper end. The lower or down-stream ends of the apron were always the most secured against scour, in the belief that a cavity would be formed below by the scouring away of the sand, but that above the currents would bring down sand and fill up any hollows that

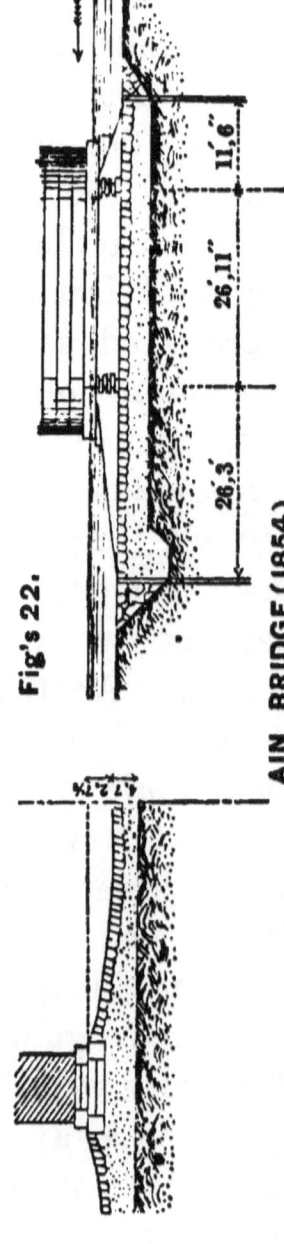

Fig's 22.

AIN BRIDGE (1854)

might have been scoured out. The investigations however, of MM. Minard and Marchall on the floods of the Loire and the Allier in 1856 indicated that the upper end of the apron is most exposed to scour and requires most protection, as the river bed close to the lower end is protected by the apron, whereas at the upper end the river bed is exposed to the full force of the current where the obstructions of the piers produce whirlpools. The apron of the Ain bridge cost £7 15s. 9d. per square yard of clear roadway above, or nearly as much as the bridge which it supports.

In certain instances the movable bed of a river has been sufficiently consolidated at the site of a work by merely a thick layer of rubble stones thrown in, giving time for the stones to take their final settlement during floods. Lastly, a movable bed can be consolidated by a wooden stockade; one of these was made, in 1820, below Amboise bridge, like the one Perronet had put down under the Orleans bridge in 1761, and both have stood perfectly.

The second case of a soil both soft and liable to scour has next to be considered. Where considerations of expense forbid going down to the solid, the following methods have been adopted :

(1) The ground is sometimes consolidated by driving a number of piles close together, or by covering it with rubble stones with or without fascine-work, so as to form a kind of superficial crust capable of bearing the structure. It is, however, generally advisable to break through the superficial stratum, and to produce a compression extending down a considerable depth by a large weight of earth, as was done for the railway bridge crossing Lake Mälar at Stockholm, where there is a thickness of 69 feet of silt under 79 feet of water. A large embankment of sand was tipped in and inclosed by sheeting, within which close rows of piles were driven, and then a water-tight caisson was lowered on a platform sunk 3¼ feet below the water, in which the foundations were commenced.

(2) Another method is to increase the bearing surface at the base by large footings, or by timber platforms, layers of concrete, bedding courses of masonry, or rubble stone.

(3) The weight of the superstructure can be diminished by forming hollow cells in the masonry, or by using iron girders instead of stone arches.

(4) In heterogeneous strata the weight must be distributed as much as possible in proportion to the bearing power at different points.

(5) It is advisable sometimes to inclose the site of the foundations with sheeting, walls, &c., not only as a protection against scour, but also to prevent the running-in of the soil from the sides when a weight is brought on it.

The Cubsac suspension bridge over the Dordogne furnishes a good example of a successful surmounting of difficulties in foundations. The suspended roadway was made as light as possible; the piers were hollow and perforated cast-iron columns, resting on a stone base supported by piles from 40 to 62 feet long, and 2 feet 7½ inches apart. The abutments and anchorage masonry were built with arched openings and light inverts, and the embankments at each end were of light limestone blocks arranged in rough arches so as to form hollow spaces in the mass.

Although in this enumeration of the different kinds of foundations bridges have generally been chosen for examples, the methods described would be applicable to other works, such as large locks, graving docks, and quay walls.

The difficulties attending the laying of lighthouse foundations, and the means adopted to surmount them, are fully detailed in descriptions of these works.

In sea works the chief difficulties are encountered above the foundations where the sea breaks against the structure, and accordingly the methods of protection adopted do not come within the limits of this Paper. But the valuable addition to the methods of foundations used for these works by the introduction of concrete blocks, which can be formed of almost any size, and deposited by divers, must not be overlooked.

The effect of pumping or hammering action referred to by Mr. W. Parkes and Sir John Coode (vol. xxxvi., Minutes of Proceedings Inst. C.E., pp. 234 and 240) is due to the immersion and emersion during the oscillation of waves. Perhaps to this cause may be partially attributed the fall of a quay wall at Vevey in the present year. This wall was founded with a base of concrete contained in metallic boxes resting on high timber piles.

M. Croizette Desnoyers has framed a classification of the methods of foundations most suitable for different depths, and also an estimate of the cost of each. These estimates, however, must be considered merely approximate, as unforeseen circumstances produce considerable variations in works of this nature.

	Depths.	Per cubic yard. s. s.
Foundations on piles after compression of the ground.....	20 to 33 feet 33 to 50 feet	12 to 18 18 to 30
Foundations by sinking wells.........	33 to 50 feet	30 to 37
Foundations by pumping...........	under 20 feet	12 to 18
26 to 33 feet	favorable circumstances unfavorable	18 to 55 61 to 73
Foundations on concrete under water.	20 to 33 ft. small amount of silt. 26 to 33 ft. large amount of silt.	18 to 37 37 to 49
Foundations by means of compressed air under favorable circumstances...		55 to 67
Foundations by means of compressed air under unfavorable conditions.........	Lorient viaduct.. Kehl bridge...... Argenteuil bridge Bordeaux bridge.	99 122 140 165

When the foundations consist of disconnected pillars or piles the above prices must be applied to the whole cubic content, including the intervals between the parts, but of course for an equal cost solid piers are the best.

For pilework foundations the square yard of base is probably a better unit than the cubic yard. Thus the foundations of the Vernon bridge, with piles from 24 to 31 feet long, and with cross timbering, concrete, and caisson, cost £14 7s. 7d. per square yard of base. According to estimates made by M. Picquenot, if the foundations had been put in by means of compressed air the cost would have been £32 15s. 7d.; with a caission, not watertight, sunk down, £13 12s. 2d.; with concrete poured into a space inclosed with sheeting, £12 15s. 7d.; and by pumping £17 3s. 2d. per square yard of base.

M. Desnoyers gives the following recommendations with regard to the choice of methods:

(1) In still water to construct the foundations by means of pumping for depths under 20 feet. In greater depths to construct ordinary works on piles if the ground is firm or has been consolidated by loading it with earth; otherwise to employ pumping, and if a permeable stratum is met with to build on it with a broad base. For important works, if the soil is watertight, it is advisable to adopt the method of pump-

ing inside a framing, carrying down the foundations to greater depths than 33 feet by the well-sinking method. If the soil, however, is permeable, dredging and concrete deposited under water must be resorted to; compressed air being employed for depths greater than 33 feet.

(2) In mid-stream compressed air mus be resorted to for foundations more than 33 feet below water. In less depths the foundations of ordinary works are put in by means of dams or watertight frames if the nature of the silt admits of pumping out the water; but if the silt is permeable a mass of concrete is poured into the site inclosed by sheeting. When, however, an important work has to be executed, it is desirable to use pumps sufficient to overcome the infiltrations. If a permeable and easily-dredged stratum lies between the hard bottom and the silt the method of a watertight casing, with a dam at the bottom, should be adopted. To complete these recommendations open cylindrical foundations

must be included. These may be resorted to, instead of compressed air, when the soil is readily dredged or watertight enough to allow of pumping, and also frequently in the place of piles or the well-sinking method. The compressed air system is essentially a last resource, applicable to a bed exposed to scour, and also either difficult to dredge or with boulders or other obstacles imbedded in it.

In conclusion, a chronological list of works is added to show at what periods the principal steps in advance were made.

The system of rubble mounds is the most ancient; and dams of earth came into vogue in the seventeenth century. In 1500–1507, the "Notre Dame" bridge at Paris was founded on piles surrounded with heavy rubble stones. In 1716 the Blois bridge was built on piles and a platform at low-water level. The method of constructing a foundation by means of an apron was introduced by Régemortes at Moulins in 1750. At the same time Labelye built the foundations of the old Westminster bridge by sinking caissons in the dredged bed of the Thames, a similar process having been adopted, in 1686, for the pier of the Tuileries bridge next the right bank of the Seine. In 1756 Des Essarts invented a saw for cutting off piles under water, which enabled a caisson to be deposited on piles for the Saumur bridge, a method thenceforward adopted for the bridges at Paris till 1857, also for the Sévres, Ivry, and Bordeaux bridges, and old Blackfriars bridge was built in the same way.

In the year 1818 Vicat discovered the properties of hydraulic mortars, and the adoption of a concrete foundation deposited inside sheeting soon followed; also the bottomless frame system with concrete at the bottom, first used by Beaudemoulin for several bridges at Paris, and adopted for the bridge over the Cher.

In 1833-40 Poirel employed for the first time artificial blocks of concrete at Algiers harbor. He also used caissons with a bottom of canvas for depositing liquid concrete *in situ*.

M. Triger first used compressed air at the Chalons coal mine in 1839; and Dr. Potts introduced his system in 1845.

The tubular method of foundations was next introduced, and under various forms is continually becoming more universally adopted. The following are the dates of some of the works for which it was used:—

Gravesend cofferdam. Mr. J. B. Redman	1842
Rochester bridge. Mr. Cubitt	1851
Saltash bridge. Mr. I. K. Brunel	1854–57
Kehl bridge. Messrs. Fleur St. Denis and Vuigner	1858–59
Charing Cross bridge. Sir J. Hawkshaw	1860
Cannon Street bridge. Sir J. Hawkshaw	1863
Victoria bridge. Sir Charles Fox	1863

In 1867 Kennard's sand-pump was used for the foundations of the Jumna bridge.

The "boring-head" was used by Mr. Leslie in 1867–70 at the Gorai bridge, and at the same time Mr. Milroy introduced his "excavator."

Lastly, between 1870 and 1873 the Americans laid the foundations of the St. Louis and East River bridges, whilst Mr. Stoney, by depositing huge blocks in the Liffey, and Mr. Dyce Cay, by depositing concrete *in situ* in large masses at the Aberdeen break-water, extended the methods of employing concrete in river and sea works.

∗ *Any book in this Catalogue sent free by mail, on receipt of price.*

VALUABLE
SCIENTIFIC BOOKS,

PUBLISHED BY

D. VAN NOSTRAND,

23 Murray Street, and 27 Warren Street,

NEW YORK.

WEISBACH. A MANUAL OF THEORETICAL MECHANICS. By Julius Weisbach, Ph. D. Translated by Eckley B. Coxe, A.M., M.E. 1100 pages and 902 wood-cut illustrations. 8vo, cloth, ... $10 00

FRANCIS. LOWELL HYDRAULIC EXPERIMENTS—being a Selection from Experiments on Hydraulic Motors, on the Flow of Water over Weirs, and in open Canals of Uniform Rectangular Section, made at Lowell, Mass. By J. B. Francis, Civil Engineer. Third edition, revised and enlarged, with 23 copper-plates, beautifully engraved, and about 100 new pages of text. 4to, cloth, ... 15 00

KIRKWOOD. ON THE FILTRATION OF RIVER WATERS, for the Supply of Cities, as practised in Europe. By James P. Kirkwood. Illustrated by 30 double-plate engravings. 4to, cloth 15 00

D. VAN NOSTRAND'S PUBLICATIONS.

FANNING. A Practical Treatise of Water Supply Engineering. Relating to the Hydrology, Hydrodynamics, and Practical Construction of Water-Works, in North America. With numerous Tables and 180 illustrations. By J. T. Fanning, C.E. 650 pages. 8vo, cloth extra, . $6 00

WHIPPLE. An Elementary Treatise on Bridge Building. By S. Whipple, C. E. New Edition. Illustrated. 8vo, cloth, 4 00

MERRILL. Iron Truss Bridges for Railroads. The Method of Calculating Strains in Trusses, with a careful comparison of the most prominent Trusses, in reference to economy in combination, etc., etc. By Bvt. Col. William E. Merrill, U. S. A., Corps of Engineers. Nine lithographed plates of illustrations. Third edition. 4to, cloth, ... 5 00

SHREVE. A Treatise on the Strength of Bridges and Roofs. Comprising the determination of Algebraic formulas for Strains in Horizontal, Inclined or Rafter, Triangular, Bowstring Lenticular and other Trusses, from fixed and moving loads, with practical applications and examples, for the use of Students and Engineers By Samuel H. Shreve, A. M., Civil Engineer. Second edition, 87 woodcut illustrations. 8vo, cloth, . . . 5 00

KANSAS CITY BRIDGE. With an Account of the Regimen of the Missouri River,—and a description of the Methods used for Founding in that River. By O. Chanute, Chief Engineer, and George Morison, Assistant Engineer. Illustrated with five lithographic views and twelve plates of plans. 4to, cloth, ... 6 00

D. VAN NOSTRAND'S PUBLICATIONS.

CLARKE. DESCRIPTION OF THE IRON RAILWAY BRIDGE Across the Mississippi River at Quincy, Illinois. By Thomas Curtis Clarke, Chief Engineer. With twenty-one lithographed Plans. 4to, cloth, . . . $7 50

ROEBLING. LONG AND SHORT SPAN RAILWAY BRIDGES. By John A. Roebling, C. E. With large copperplate engravings of plans and views. Imperial folio, cloth, . 25 00

DUBOIS. THE NEW METHOD OF GRAPHICAL STATICS. By A. J. Dubois, C. E., Ph. D. 60 illustrations. 8vo, cloth. 2 00

EDDY. NEW CONSTRUCTIONS IN GRAPHICAL STATICS. By Prof. Henry B. Eddy, C. E Ph. D. Illustrated by ten engravings in text, and nine folding plates. 8vo, cloth, 1 50

BOW. A TREATISE ON BRACING—with its application to Bridges and other Structures of Wood or Iron. By Robert Henry Bow, C. E. 156 illustrations on stone. 8vo, cloth, 1 50

STONEY. THE THEORY OF STRAINS IN GIRDERS —and Similar Structures—with Observations on the Application of Theory to Practice, and Tables of Strength and other Properties of Materials. By Bindon B. Stoney, B. A. New and Revised Edition, with numerous illustrations. Royal 8vo, 664 pp., cloth, ... 12 50

HENRICI. SKELETON STRUCTURES, especially in their Application to the building of Steel and Iron Bridges. By Olaus Henrici. 8vo, cloth, ... 1 50

KING. LESSONS AND PRACTICAL NOTES ON STEAM. The Steam Engine, Propellers, &c., &c., for Young Engineers. By the late W. R. King, U. S. N., revised by Chief-Engineer J. W. King, U. S. Navy. 19th edition. 8vo, cloth, ... 2 00

2

D. VAN NOSTRAND'S PUBLICATIONS.

AUCHINCLOSS. APPLICATION OF THE SLIDE VALVE and Link Motion to Stationary, Portable, Locomotive and Marine Engines. By William S Auchincloss. Designed as a hand-book for Mechanical Engineers. With 37 wood-cuts and 21 lithographic plates, with copper-plate engraving of the Travel Scale. Sixth edition. 8vo, cloth, ... $3 00

BURGH. MODERN MARINE ENGINEERING, applied to Paddle and Screw Propulsion. Consisting of 36 Colored Plates, 259 Practical Wood-cut Illustrations, and 403 pages of Descriptive Matter, the whole being an exposition of the present practice of the following firms: Messrs. J. Penn & Sons; Messrs. Maudslay, Sons & Field; Messrs. James Watt & Co.; Messrs. J. & G. Rennie. Messrs. R. Napier & Sons; Messrs J. & W. Dudgeon; Messrs. Ravenhill & Hodgson; Messrs Humphreys & Tenant; Mr J. T. Spencer, and Messrs. Forrester & Co. By N P. Burgh. Engineer. One thick 4to vol., cloth, $25.00; half morocco, 30 00

BACON. A TREATISE ON THE RICHARD'S STEAM-ENGINE INDICATOR — with directions for its use. By Charles T. Porter. Revised, with notes and large additions as developed by American Practice; with an Appendix containing useful formulæ and rules for Engineers. By F. W. Bacon, M. E. Illustrated Second edition. 12mo. Cloth $1.00; morocco, ... 1 50

ISHERWOOD. ENGINEERING PRECEDENTS FOR STEAM MACHINERY. By B. F. Isherwood, Chief Engineer, U. S. Navy. With illustrations. Two vols. in one. 8vo, cloth, 2 50

STILLMAN. THE STEAM ENGINE INDICATOR —and the Improved Manometer Steam and Vacuum Gauges—their utility and application. By Paul Stillman. New edition. 12mo, cloth, ... 1 00

MacCORD. A Practical Treatise on the Slide Valve, by Eccentrics—examining by methods the action of the Eccentric upon the Slide Valve, and explaining the practical processes of laying out the movements, adapting the valve for its various duties in the steam-engine. By C. W. Mac Cord, A. M., Professor of Mechanical Drawing, Stevens' Institute of Technology, Hoboken, N. J. Illustrated. 4to, cloth, ... $3 00

PORTER. A Treatise on the Richards' Steam-Engine Indicator, and the Development and Application of Force in the Steam-Engine. By Charles T. Porter. Third edition, revised and enlarged. Illustrated. 8vo, cloth, . . . 3 50

McCULLOCH. A Treatise on the Mechanical Theory of Heat, and its Applications to the Steam-Engine. By Prof. R. S. McCulloch, of the Washington and Lee University, Lexington. Va. 8vo. cloth, ... 3 50

VAN BUREN. Investigations of Formulas—for the Strength of the Iron parts of Steam Machinery. By J. D. Van Buren, Jr., C. E. Illustrated. 8vo, cloth, . 2 00

STUART. How to Become a Successful Engineer. Being Hints to Youths intending to adopt the Profession. By Bernard Stuart, Engineer Sixth edition 18mo, boards, ... 50

SHIELDS A Treatise on Engineering Construction. Embracing Discussions of the Principles involved, and Descriptions of the Material employed in Tunneling, Bridging, Canal and Road Building, etc., etc. By J. E. Shields, C. E. 12mo. cloth, 1 50

D. VAN NOSTRAND'S PUBLICATIONS.

WEYRAUCH. STRENGTH AND CALCULATION OF DIMENSIONS OF IRON AND STEEL CONSTRUCTIONS. Translated from the German of J. J. Weyrauch, Ph. D., with four folding Plates. 12mo, cloth, . . . $1 00

STUART. THE NAVAL DRY DOCKS OF THE UNITED STATES. By Charles B. Stuart, Engineer in Chief, U. S. Navy. Twenty-four engravings on steel. Fourth edition. 4to, cloth, ... 6 00

COLLINS. THE PRIVATE BOOK OF USEFUL ALLOYS, and Memoranda for Goldsmiths, Jewellers, etc. By James E. Collins. 18mo, flexible cloth, ... 50

TUNNER. A TREATISE ON ROLL-TURNING FOR THE MANUFACTURE OF IRON. By Peter Tunner Translated by John B. Pearse. With numerous wood-cuts, 8vo, and a folio Atlas of 10 lithographed plates of Rolls, Measurements, &c. Cloth, . . 10 00

GRUNER. THE MANUFACTURE OF STEEL. By M. L. Gruner. Translated from the French, by Lenox Smith, A.M., E.M.; with an Appendix on the Bessemer Process in the United States, by the translator. Illustrated by lithographed drawings and wood-cuts. 8vo, cloth, ... 3 50

BARBA. THE USE OF STEEL IN CONSTRUCTION. Methods of Working, Applying, and Testing Plates and Bars. By J. Barba. Translated from the French, with a Preface by A. L. Holley, P.B. Illustrated. 12mo, cloth, 1 50

BELL. CHEMICAL PHENOMENA OF IRON SMELTING. An Experimental and Practical Examination of the Circumstances which Determine the Capacity of the Blast Furnace, the Temperature of the Air, and the Proper Condition of the Materials to be operated upon. By I. Lowthian Bell. 8vo, cloth, ... 6 00

D. VAN NOSTRAND'S PUBLICATIONS.

WARD. STEAM FOR THE MILLION. A Popular Treatise on Steam and its Application to the Useful Arts, especially to Navigation. By J. H. Ward, Commander U. S. Navy. 8vo, cloth. $1 00

CLARK. A MANUAL OF RULES, TABLES AND DATA FOR MECHANICAL ENGINEERS. Based on the most recent investigations. By Dan. Kinnear Clark. Illustrated with numerous diagrams. 1012 pages. 8vo. Cloth, $7 50; half morocco, ... 10 00

JOYNSON. THE METALS USED IN CONSTRUCTION: Iron, Steel, Bessemer Metals, etc, By F. H. Joynson. Illustrated. 12mo, cloth, ... 75

DODD. DICTIONARY OF MANUFACTURES, MINING, MACHINERY, AND THE INDUSTRIAL ARTS. By George Dodd. 12mo, cloth, 1 50

VON COTTA. TREATISE ON ORE DEPOSITS. By Bernhard Von Cotta, Freiburg, Saxony. Translated from the second German ed., by Frederick Prime, Jr., and revised by the author. With numerous illustrations. 8vo, cloth, ... 4 00

PLATTNER. MANUAL OF QUALITATIVE AND QUANTITATIVE ANALYSIS WITH THE BLOW-PIPE. From the last German edition. Revised and enlarged. By Prof. Th. Richter, o the Royal Saxon Mining Academy. Translated by Professor H. B. Cornwall. With eighty-seven wood-cuts and lithographic plate. Third edition, revised. 568 pp. 8vo, cloth, ... 5 00

PLYMPTON. THE BLOW-PIPE: A Guide to its Use in the Determination of Salts and Minerals. Compiled from various sources, by George W. Plympton, C. E., A. M., Professor of Physical Science in the Polytechnic Institute, Brooklyn, N. Y. 12mo, cloth, 1 50

D. VAN NOSTRAND'S PUBLICATIONS.

JANNETTAZ. A GUIDE TO THE DETERMINATION OF ROCKS; being an Introduction to Lithology. By Edward Jannettaz, Docteur des Sciences. Translated from the French by G. W. Plympton, Professor of Physical Science at Brooklyn Polytechnic Institute. 12mo, cloth, ... $1 50

MOTT. A PRACTICAL TREATISE ON CHEMISTRY (Qualitative and Quantitative Analysis), Stoichiometry, Blowpipe Analysis, Mineralogy, Assaying, Pharmaceutical Preparations. Human Secretions, Specific Gravities, Weights and Measures, etc., etc., etc. By Henry A. Mott, Jr., E. M., Ph. D. 650 pp. 8vo, cloth, ... 6 00

PYNCHON. INTRODUCTION TO CHEMICAL PHYSICS; Designed for the Use of Academies, Colleges, and High Schools. Illustrated with numerous engravings, and containing copious experiments, with directions for preparing them. By Thomas Ruggles Pynchon, D. D., M. A., President of Trinity College, Hartford. New edition, revised and enlarged. Crown 8vo, cloth, . . . 3 00

PRESCOTT. CHEMICAL EXAMINATION OF ALCOHOLIC LIQUORS. A Manual of the Constituents of the Distilled Spirits and Fermented Liquors of Commerce, and their Qualitative and Quantitative Determinations. By Alb. B. Prescott, Prof. of Chemistry, University of Michigan. 12mo, cloth, . 1 50

ELIOT AND STORER. A COMPENDIOUS MANUAL OF QUALITATIVE CHEMICAL ANALYSIS. By Charles W. Eliot and Frank H. Storer. Revised, with the co-operation of the Authors, by William Ripley Nichols, Professor of Chemistry in the Massachusetts Institute of Technology. New edition, revised. Illustrated. 12mo, cloth, ... 1 50

D. VAN NOSTRAND'S PUBLICATIONS.

NAQUET. LEGAL CHEMISTRY. A Guide to the Detection of Poisons, Falsification of Writings, Adulteration of Alimentary and Pharmaceutical Substances; Analysis of Ashes, and Examination of Hair, Coins, Fire-arms and Stains, as Applied to Chemical Jurisprudence. For the Use of Chemists, Physicians, Lawyers, Pharmacists, and Experts. Translated, with additions, including a List of Books and Memoirs on Toxicology, etc., from the French of A. Naquet, by J. P. Battershall, Ph. D.; with a Preface by C. F. Chandler, Ph. D., M. D., LL. D. Illustrated. 12mo, cloth, ... $2 00

PRESCOTT. OUTLINES OF PROXIMATE ORGANIC ANALYSIS for the Identification, Separation, and Quantitative Determination of the more commonly occurring Organic Compounds. By Albert B. Prescott, Professor of Chemistry, University of Michigan. 12mo, cloth, ... 1 75

DOUGLAS AND PRESCOTT. QUALITATIVE CHEMICAL ANALYSIS. A Guide in the Practical Study of Chemistry, and in the work of Analysis. By S. H. Douglas and A. B. Prescott; Professors in the University of Michigan. Second edition, revised. 8vo, cloth, ... 3 50

RAMMELSBERG. GUIDE TO A COURSE OF QUANTITATIVE CHEMICAL ANALYSIS, ESPECIALLY OF MINERALS AND FURNACE PRODUCTS. Illustrated by Examples. By C. F. Rammelsberg. Translated by J. Towler, M. D. 8vo, cloth, ... 2 25

BEILSTEIN. AN INTRODUCTION TO QUALITATIVE CHEMICAL ANALYSIS. By F. Beilstein. Third edition. Translated by I. J. Osbun. 12mo. cloth, ... 75

POPE. A Hand-book for Electricians and Operators. By Frank L. Pope. Ninth edition. Revised and enlarged, and fully illustrated. 8vo, cloth, ... 2 00

D. VAN NOSTRAND'S PUBLICATIONS.

SABINE. HISTORY AND PROGRESS OF THE ELECTRIC TELEGRAPH, with Descriptions of some of the Apparatus. By Robert Sabine, C. E. Second edition. 12mo, cloth, . . . $1 25

DAVIS AND RAE. HAND BOOK OF ELECTRICAL DIAGRAMS AND CONNECTIONS. By Charles H. Davis and Frank B. Rae. Illustrated with 32 full-page illustrations. Second edition. Oblong 8vo, cloth extra, . . . 2 00

HASKINS. THE GALVANOMETER, AND ITS USES. A Manual for Electricians and Students. By C. H. Haskins. Illustrated. Pocket form, morocco, ... 1 50

LARRABEE. CIPHER AND SECRET LETTER AND TELEGRAPAIC CODE, with Hogg's Improvements. By C. S. Larrabee. 18mo, flexible cloth, ... 1 00

GILLMORE PRACTICAL TREATISE ON LIMES, HYDRAULIC CEMENT, AND MORTARS. By Q. A. Gillmore, Lt.-Col. U. S. Engineers, Brevet Major-General U. S. Army. Fifth edition, revised and enlarged. 8vo, cloth, 4 00

GILLMORE. COIGNET BETON AND OTHER ARTIFICIAL STONE. By Q. A. Gillmore, Lt. Col. U. S. Engineers, Brevet Major-General U. S. Army. Nine plates, views, etc. 8vo, cloth, ... 2 50

GILLMORE. A PRACTICAL TREATISE ON THE CONSTRUCTION OF ROADS, STREETS, AND PAVEMENTS. By Q. A. Gillmore, Lt.-Col. U. S. Engineers, Brevet Major-General U. S. Army. Seventy illustrations. 12mo, clo., 2 00

GILLMORE. REPORT ON STRENGTH OF THE BUILDING STONES IN THE UNITED STATES, etc. 8vo, cloth, ... 1 00

HOLLEY. AMERICAN AND EUROPEAN RAILWAY PRACTICE, in the Economical Generation of Steam. By Alexander L. Holley. B. P. With 77 lithographed plates. Folio, cloth, 12 00

D. VAN NOSTRAND'S PUBLICATIONS.

HAMILTON. USEFUL INFORMATION FOR RAILWAY MEN. Compiled by W. G. Hamilton, Engineer. Seventh edition, revised and enlarged. 577 pages. Pocket form, morocco, gilt, ... , . $2 00

STUART. THE CIVIL AND MILITARY ENGINEERS OF AMERICA. By General Charles B. Stuart, Author of "Naval Dry Docks of the United States," etc., etc. With nine finely-executed Portraits on steel, of eminent Engineers, and illustrated by Engravings of some of the most important and original works constructed in America. 8vo, cloth, ... 5 00

ERNST. A MANUAL OF PRACTICAL MILITARY ENGINEERING. Prepared for the use of the Cadets of the U. S. Military Academy, and for Engineer Troops. By Capt. O. H. Ernst, Corps of Engineers, Instructor in Practical Military Engineering, U. S. Military Academy. 193 wood-cuts and 3 lithographed plates. 12mo, cloth, . . 5 00

SIMMS. A TREATISE ON THE PRINCIPLES AND PRACTICE OF LEVELLING, showing its application to purposes of Railway Engineering and the Construction of Roads, etc. By Frederick W. Simms, C. E. From the fifth London edition, revised and corrected, with the addition of Mr. Law's Practical Examples for Setting-out Railway Curves. Illustrated with three lithographic plates, and numerous wood-cuts. 8vo, cloth, ... 2 50

JEFFERS. NAUTICAL SURVEYING. By William N. Jeffers, Captain U. S. Navy. Illustrated with 9 copperplates, and 31 wood-cut illustrations. 8vo, cloth, ... 5 00

THE PLANE TABLE. ITS USES IN TOPOGRAPHICAL SURVEYING. From the papers of the U. S. Coast Survey. 8vo, cloth, . . 2 00

D. VAN NOSTRAND'S PUBLICATIONS.

A TEXT-BOOK ON SURVEYING, Projections, and Portable Instruments, for the use of the Cadet Midshipmen, at the U. S. Naval Academy. 9 lithographed plates, and several wood-cuts. 8vo, cloth, . . $2 00

CHAUVENET. New Method of Correcting Lunar Distances. By Wm. Chauvenet, LL.D. 8vo, cloth, ... 2 00

BURT. Key to the Solar Compass, and Surveyor's Companion; comprising all the Rules necessary for use in the Field. By W. A. Burt, U. S. Deputy Surveyor. Second edition. Pocket-book form, tuck, . 2 50

HOWARD. Earthwork Mensuration on the Basis of the Prismoidal Formulæ. Containing simple and labor-saving method of obtaining Prismoidal Contents directly from End Areas. Illustrated by Examples, and accompanied by Plain Rules for practical uses. By Conway R. Howard, Civil Engineer, Richmond, Va. Illustrated. 8vo, cloth, ... 1 50

MORRIS. Easy Rules for the Measurement of Earthworks, by means of the Prismoidal Formulæ. By Elwood Morris, Civil Engineer. 78 illustrations. 8vo, cloth, 1 50

CLEVENGER. A Treatise on the Method of Government Surveying, as prescribed by the U. S. Congress and Commissioner of the General Land Office. With complete Mathematical, Astronomical, and Practical Instructions for the use of the U. S. Surveyors in the Field. By S. V. Clevenger, U. S. Deputy Surveyor. Illustrated. Pocket form, morocco, gilt, . . . 2 50

HEWSON. Principles and Practice of Embanking Lands from River Floods, as applied to the Levees of the Mississipi. By William Hewson, Civil Engineer. 8vo, cloth, ... 2 00

D. VAN NOSTRAND'S PUBLICATIONS.

MINIFIE. A Text-Book of Geometrical Drawing, for the use of Mechanics and Schools. With Illustrations for Drawing Plans, Elevations of Buildings and Machinery. With over 200 diagrams on steel. By William Minifie, Architect. Ninth edition. Royal 8vo, cloth, ... $4 00

MINIFIE Geometrical Drawing. Abridged from the octavo edition, for the use of Schools. Illustrated with 48 steel plates. New edition, enlarged. 12mo, cloth, 2 00

FREE HAND DRAWING. A Guide to Ornamental, Figure, and Landscape Drawing. By an Art Student. Profusely illustrated. 18mo, boards, ... 50

AXON. The Mechanic's Friend. A Collection of Receipts and Practical Suggestions, relating to Aquaria—Bronzing—Cements—Drawing—Dyes—Electricity—Gilding—Glass-working—Glues—Horology—Lacquers—Locomotives—Magnetism—Metalworking—Modelling—Photography—Pyrotechny—Railways—Solders—Steam-Engine—Telegraphy—Taxidermy—Varnishes—Waterproofing-and Miscellaneous Tools, Instruments, Machines, and Processes connected with the Chemical and Mechanical Arts. By William E. Axon, M.R.S.L. 12mo, cloth. 300 illustrations, . . . 1 50

HARRISON. Mechanics' Tool Book, with Practical Rules and Suggestions, for the use of Machinists, Iron Workers, and others. By W. B. Harrison. 44 illustrations. 12mo, cloth 1 50

JOYNSON. The Mechanic's and Student's Guide in the designing and Construction of General Machine Gearing. Edited by Francis H. Joynson. With 18 folded plates. 8vo, cloth 2 00

D. VAN NOSTRAND'S PUBLICATIONS.

RANDALL. QUARTZ OPERATOR'S HAND-BOOK. By P. M. Randall. New Edition. Revised and Enlarged. Fully illustrated. 12mo, cloth, ... $2 00

SILVERSMITH. A PRACTICAL HAND-BOOK FOR MINERS, METALLURGISTS, and Assayers. By Julius Silversmith. Fourth Edition. Illustrated. 12mo, cloth, ... 3 00

BARNES. SUBMARINE WARFARE, DEFENSIVE AND OFFENSIVE. Descriptions of the various forms of Torpedoes, Submarine Batteries and Torpedo Boats actually used in War. Methods of Ignition by Machinery, Contact Fuzes, and Electricity, and a full account of experiments made to determine the Explosive Force of Gunpowder under Water. Also a discussion of the Offensive Torpedo system; its effect upon Iron-clad Ship systems, and influence upon future Naval Wars. By Lieut.-Com. John S. Barnes, U. S. N. With 20 lithographic plates and many wood-cuts. 8vo, cloth, 5 00

FOSTER. SUBMARINE BLASTING, in Boston Harbor, Mass. Removal of Tower and Corwin Rocks. By John G. Foster, U. S. Eng. and Bvt. Major General U. S. Army. With seven Plates. 4to, cloth, 3 50

MOWBRAY. TRI-NITRO-GLYCERINE, as applied in the Hoosac Tunnel, and to Submarine Blasting, Torpedoes, Quarrying, etc. Illustrated. 8vo, cloth, . . . 3 00

WILLIAMSON. ON THE USE OF THE BAROMETER ON SURVEYS AND RECONNAISSANCES. Part I.—Meteorology in its Connection with Hypsometry. Part II.—Barometric Hypsometry. By R. S. Williamson, Bvt. Lt.-Col. U.S.A., Major Corps of Engineers. With illustrative tables and engravings. 4to, cloth, ... 15 00

D. VAN NOSTRAND'S PUBLICATIONS.

WILLIAMSON. PRACTICAL TABLES IN METEOROLOGY AND HYPSOMETRY, in connection with the use of the Barometer By Col. R. S. Williamson, U. S. A. 4to, flexible cloth, $2 50

BUTLER. PROJECTILES AND RIFLED CANNON A Critical Discussion of the Principal Systems of Rifling and Projectiles, with Practical Suggestions for their Improvement. By Capt. John S. Butler, Ordnance Corps, U. S. A. 36 Plates. 4to, cloth, . . 7 50

BENET ELECTRO-BALLISTIC MACHINES, and the Schultz Chronoscope. By Lt.-Col S. V Benet, Chief of Ordnance U. S. A. Second edition, illustrated. 4to, cloth, . 3 00

MICHAELIS. THE LE BOULENGE CHRONOGRAPH. With three lithographed folding plates of illustrations. By Bvt. Captian O. E. Michaelis, Ordnance Corpse, U. S. A. 4to, cloth, ... 3 00

NUGENT. TTEATISE ON OPTICS; or Light and Sight, theoretically and practically treated; with the application to Fine Art and Industrial Pursuits. By E. Nugent. With 103 illustrations. 12mo, cloth, . . . 1 50

PEIRCE. SYSTEM OF ANALYTIC MECHANICS. By Benjamin Peirce, Professor of Astronomy and Mathematics in Harvard University. 4to cloth, ... 10 00

CRAIG. WEIGHTS AND MEASURES. An Account of the Decimal System, with Tables of Conversion for Commercial and Scientific Uses. By B. F. Craig, M. D. Square 32mo, limp cloth, ... 50

ALEXANDER. UNIVERSAL DICTIONARY OF WEIGHTS AND MEASURES, Ancient and Modern, reduced to the standards of the United States of America. By J H. Alexander. New edition. 8vo, cloth, . . 3 50

D. VAN NOSTRAND'S PUBLICATIONS.

ELLIOT. EUROPEAN LIGHT-HOUSE SYSTEMS. Being a Report of a Tour of Inspection made in 1873. By Major George H. Elliot, U. S. Engineers. 51 engravings and 21 wood-cuts. 8vo, cloth, ... $5 00

SWEET. SPECIAL REPORT ON COAL. By S. H. Sweet. With Maps. 8vo, cloth, . . 3 00

COLBURN. GAS WORKS OF LONDON. By Zerah Colburn. 12mo, boards, ... 60

WALKER. NOTES ON SCREW PROPULSION, its Rise and History. By Capt. W. H. Walker, U. S. Navy. 8vo, cloth, ... 75

POOK. METHOD OF PREPARING THE LINES AND DRAUGHTING VESSELS PROPELLED BY SAIL OR STEAM, including a Chapter on Laying-off on the Mould-loft Floor. By Samuel M. Pook, Naval Constructor. Illustrated. 8vo, cloth, ... 5 00

SAELTZER. TREATISE ON ACOUSTICS in connection with Ventilation. By Alexander Saeltzer. 12mo, cloth, ... 2 00

EASLIE A HAND-BOOK FOR THE USE OF CONTACTORS, Builders, Architects, Engineers, Timber Merchants, etc., with information for drawing up Designs and Estimates. 250 illustrations. 8vo, cloth, . . . 1 50

SCHUMANN. A MANUAL OF HEATING AND VENTILATION IN ITS PRACTICAL APPLICATION for the use of Engineers and Architects, embracing a series of Tables and Formulæ for dimensions of heating, flow and return Pipes for steam and hot water boilers, flues, etc, etc. By F Schumann, C. E., U. S. Treasury Department 12mo. Illustrated *In press*

TONER. DICTIONARY OF ELEVATIONS AND CLIMATIC REGISTER OF THE UNITED STATES. By J. M. Toner, M D 8vo. Paper, $3.00; cloth. 3 75

D. VAN NOSTRAND'S PUBLICATIONS.

WANKLYN. MILK ANALYSIS. A Practical Treatise on the Examination of Milk, and its Derivatives, Cream, Butter, and Cheese. By J. Alfred Wanklyn, M.R.C.S. 12mo, cloth, ... $1 00

RICE & JOHNSON. ON A NEW METHOD OF OBTAINING THE DIFFERENTIALS OF FUNCTIONS, with especial reference to the Newtonian Conception of Rates or Velocities. By J. Minot Rice, Prof. of Mathematics, U. S. Navy, and W. Woolsey Johnson, Prof. of Mathemathics, St. John's College. Annapolis. 12mo, paper. . . . 50

COFFIN. NAVIGATION AND NAUTICAL ASTRONOMY. Prepared for the use of the U. S. Naval Academy. By J. H. C. Coffin, Professor of Astronomy, Navigation and Surveying; with 52 wood-cut illustrations. Fifth edition. 12mo, cloth. . . 3 50

CLARK. THEORETICAL NAVIGATION AND NAUTICAL ASTRONOMY. By Lewis Clark, Lieut.-Commander, U. S Navy Illustrated with 41 wood-cuts, including the Vernier. 8vo, cloth, . . 3 00

ROGERS. THE GEOLOGY OF PENNSYLVANIA. By Henry Darwin Rogers, late State Geologist of Pennsylvania. 3 vols 4to, with Portfolio of Maps. Cloth, ... 30 00

IN PREPARATION.

WEISBACH. MECHANICS OF ENGINEERING, APPLIED MECHANICS; containing Arches, Bridges, Foundations, Hydraulics, Steam Engine, and other Prime Movers, &c., &c. Translated from the latest German Edition 2 vols., 8vo.

Van Nostrand's Science Series.

It is the intention of the Publisher of this Series to issue them at intervals of about a month. They will be put up in a uniform, neat, and attractive form, 18mo, fancy boards. The subjects will be of an eminently scientific nature, and embrace as wide a range of topics as possible,—all of the highest character.

Price, 50 Cents Each.

I. CHIMNEYS FOR FURNACES, FIRE-PLACES, AND STEAM BOILERS. By R. Armstrong, C. E.

II. STEAM BOILER EXPLOSIONS. By Zerah Colburn.

III. PRACTICAL DESIGNING OF RETAINING WALLS. By Arthur Jacob, A. B. Illustrated.

IV. PROPORTIONS OF PINS USED IN BRIDGES. By Charles E. Bender, C. E. Illustrated.

V. VENTILATION OF BUILDINGS. By W. F. Butler. Illustrated.

VI. ON THE DESIGNING AND CONSTRUCTION OF STORAGE RESERVOIRS. By Arthur Jacob. Illustrated.

VII. SURCHARGED AND DIFFERENT FORMS OF RETAINING WALLS. By James S. Tate, C. E.

VIII. A TREATISE ON THE COMPOUND ENGINE. By John Turnbull. Illustrated.

IX. FUEL. By C. William Siemens. To which is appended the value of ARTIFICIAL FUELS AS COMPARED WITH COAL. By John Wormald, C. E.

X. COMPOUND ENGINES. Translated from the French of A. Mallet. Illustrated.

XI. THEORY OF ARCHES. By Prof. W. Allan, of the Washington and Lee College. Illustrated.

D. VAN NOSTRAND'S PUBLICATIONS.

XII. A Practical Theory of Voussoir Arches. By William Cain, C.E. Illustrated.

XIII. A Practical Treatise on the Gases Met with in Coal Mines. By the late J. J. Atkinson, Government Inspector of Mines for the County of Durham, England.

XIV. Friction of Air in Mines. By J. J. Atkinson, author of "A Practical Treatise on the Gases met with in Coal Mines."

XV. Skew Arches. By Prof. E. W. Hyde, C. E. Illustrated with numerous engravings, and three folded Plates.

XVI. A Graphic Method for Solving Certain Algebraic Equations. By Prof. George L. Vose. Illustrated.

XVII. Water and Water Supply. By Prof. W. H. Corfield, M. A., of the University College, London.

XVIII. Sewerage and Sewage Utilization. By Prof. W. H. Corfield, M. A., of the University College, London.

XIX. Strength of Beams Under Transverse Loads. By Prof. W. Allan, author of "Theory of Arches." Illustrated.

XX. Bridge and Tunnel Centres. By John B. McMasters, C. E. Illustrated.

XXI. Safety Valves. By Richard H. Buel, C. E. Illustrated.

XXII. High Masonry Dams. By John B. McMasters, C. E. Illustrated.

XXIII. The Fatigue of Metals, under Repeated Strains; with various Tables of Results of Experiments. From the German of Prof. Ludwig Spangenberg. With a Preface by S. H. Shreve, A. M. Illustrated.

XXIV. A Practical Treatise on the Teeth of Wheels, with the theory of the use of Robinson's Odontograph. By S. W. Robinson, Prof. of Mechanical Engineering, Illinois Industrial University.

D. VAN NOSTRAND'S PUBLICATIONS.

XXV. THEORY AND CALCULATIONS OF CONTINUOUS BRIDGES. By Mansfield Merriman, C. E. Illustrated.

XXVI. PRACTICAL TREATISE ON THE PROPERTIES OF CONTINUOUS BRIDGES. By Charles Bender, C. E.

XXVII. ON BOILER INCRUSTATION AND CORROSION. By F. S. Rowan.

XXVIII. ON TRANSMISSION OF POWER BY WIRE ROPE. By Albert W. Stahl.

XXIX. INJECTORS; their Theory and Use. Translated from the French of M. Leon Pouchet.

XXX. TERRESTRIAL MAGNETISM AND THE MAGNETISM OF IRON VESSELS. By Prof. Fairman Rogers.

XXXI. THE SANITARY CONDITION OF DWELLING HOUSES IN TOWN AND COUNTRY. By George E. Waring, Jr., Consulting Engineer for Sanitary and Agricultural Works. Illustrated.

XXXII. CABLE MAKING FOR SUSPENSION BRIDGES, as exemplified in the Construction of the East River Bridge. By Wilhelm Hildenbrand, C. E.

. *Other Works in Preparation for this Series.*

THE UNIVERSITY SERIES.

No. 1.—ON THE PHYSICAL BASIS OF LIFE. By Prof. T. H. Huxley, LL. D., F. R. S. With an introduction by a Professor in Yale College. 12mo, 36 pp. Paper covers, 25 cents.

No. 2.—THE CORELATION OF VITAL AND PHYSICAL FORCES. By Prof. George F. Barker, M. D., of Yale College. 36 pp. Paper covers, 25 cents.

No. 3.—AS REGARDS PROTOPLASM, in relation to Prof. Huxley's Physical Basis of Life. By J. Hutchinson Stirling, F. R. C. S. 72 pp., 25 cents.

No. 4.—ON THE HYPOTHESIS OF EVOLUTION, Physical and Metaphysical. By Prof. Edward D. Cope. 12mo, 72 pp. Paper covers, 25 cents.

No. 5.—SCIENTIFIC ADDRESSES :—1. On the Methods and Tendencies of Physical Investigation. 2. On Haze and Dust. 3. On the Scientific Use of the Imagination. By Prof. John Tyndall, F. R. S. 12mo, 74 pp. Paper covers, 25 cents. Flex. cloth, 50 cents.

No. 6.—NATURAL SELECTION AS APPLIED TO MAN. By Alfred Russel Wallace. This pamphlet treats (1) of the Development of Human Races under the Law of Selection ; (2) the Limits of Natural Selection as applied to Man. 54 pp., 25 cents.

No. 7.—SPECTRUM ANALYSIS. Three Lectures by Profs. Roscoe, Huggins and Lockyer. Finely illustrated. 88 pp. Paper covers, 25 cents.

No. 8.—THE SUN. A sketch of the present state of scientific opinion as regards this body. By Prof. C. A. Young, Ph. D., of Dartmouth College. 58 pp. Paper covers, 25 cents.

No. 9.—THE EARTH A GREAT MAGNET. By A. M. Mayer, Ph. D., of Stephens' Institute. 72 pages. Paper covers, 25 cents. Flexible cloth, 50 cents.

No. 10.—MYSTERIES OF THE VOICE AND EAR. By Prof. O. N. Rood, Columbia College, New York. Beautifully illustrated. 38 pp. Paper covers, 25 cents.

VAN NOSTRAND'S
Eclectic Engineering Magazine,
LARGE 8vo, MONTHLY

Terms, $5.00 per annum, in advance.

Single Copies, 50 Cents.

First Number was issued January 1, 1869.

VAN NOSTRAND'S MAGAZINE consists of Articles, Original and Selected, as also Matter condensed from all the Engineering Serial Publications of Europe and America.

SEVENTEEN VOLUMES NOW COMPLETE.

NOTICE TO NEW SUBSCRIBERS.—Persons commencing their subscriptions with the Eighteenth Volume (January, 1878), and who are desirous of possessing the work from its commencement, will be supplied with Volumes I to XVII, inclusive, neatly bound in cloth, for $45.00. Half morocco, $70.50. Sent free by mail or express on receipt of price.

NOTICE TO CLUBS.—An extra copy will be supplied, gratis, to every Club of five subscribers, at $5.00 each, sent in one remittance.

This magazine is made up of copious reprints from the leading scientific periodicals of Europe, together with original articles. It is extremely well edited and cannot fail to prove a valuable adjunct in promoting the engineering skill of this country.—*New York World.*

No person intererested in any of the various branches of the engineering profession can afford to be without this magazine.—*Telegrapher.*

The most useful engineering periodical extant, at least for American readers.—*Chemical News.*

As an abstract and condensation of current engineering literature this magazine will be of great value, and as it is the first enterprise of the kind in this country, it ought to have the cordial support of the engineering profession and all interested in mechanical or scientific progress.—*Iron Age.*

www.ingramcontent.com/pod-product-compliance
Lightning Source LLC
Chambersburg PA
CBHW021940160426
43195CB00011B/1160